WRITERS AND '

ISOBEL ARN
General

C000212039

IVOR GURNEY

Ivor Gurney (fourth from right, back row) with his Battalion Regiment Band in 1915.

Ivor Gurney (far left) at camp with Gloster comrades.

WW

IVOR GURNEY

JOHN LUCAS

[handwritten inscription:]
*for Andrew ~~Lucas~~ Lim(?)
with much love
John
Sept '01*

Northcote House
in association with the
British Council

First published in 2001 by Northcote House Publishers Ltd, Horndon, Tavistock, Devon, PL19 9NQ, United Kingdom.
Tel: +44 (01822) 810066 Fax: +44 (01822) 810034.

British Library Cataloguing-in-Publication Data
A catalogue record for this book is available from the British Library

ISBN 0-7463-0887-6

Typeset by PDQ Typesetting, Newcastle-under-Lyme
Printed and bound in the United Kingdom by
The Baskerville Press Ltd, Salisbury, Wiltshire, SP2 7QB

for Ross Bradshaw

'Authority forgotten, all goes well
In this our Commonwealth...'
Ivor Gurney, 'On Rest'

Contents

Prefatory Note

Only two collections of Ivor Gurney's poems were published
during his lifetime. *Severn & Somme* was first published in 1917
and reprinted two years later. *War's Embers* was also published in
1919, but to disappointing reviews and poor sales. Gurney tried to
interest his publishers, Sidgwick & Jackson, in further collections,
notably one that became known as *80 Poems or So*, which he
offered them twice in 1922. However, like all his other would-be
collections, *80 Poems or So* remained unpublished until the 1990s.
During that decade R. K. R. Thornton and George Walter brought
out important editions of the two published collections, as well as
80 Poems or So, Best Poems and the Book of Five Makings, and finally
Rewards of Wonder. In between, there had been two selections of
Gurney's poems by Edmund Blunden (1954) and Leonard Clarke
(1973), and then, in 1982, and beginning the upturn of Gurney's
posthumous reputation, P. J. Kavanagh's *Collected Poems*. Although
Thornton and Walter have had cause to revise the dating and text
of some of the poems Kavanagh includes, as well as putting into
print poems he excluded or was unaware of (for *Collected* certainly
doesn't mean *Complete*), anyone who cares about Gurney owes
Kavanagh a huge debt, not least for his magnificent Introduction.
I can recall very clearly Derek Mahon phoning me to ask whether
I'd like to review the edition for the *New Statesman*, of which I was
then poetry reviewer as Derek was poetry editor. I wasn't all that
keen, I told him. I'd read Blunden's selection and I couldn't
imagine there'd be much in the Kavanagh that would cause me to
revise my opinion of Gurney as a minor Georgian. 'Still,' I said,
'send it along and I'll see if there's anything worth saying about
him.'

Two days later *Collected Poems of Ivor Gurney* arrived. I sat in the
garden, turning over pages, looking at verses that were, yes, more

or less as I remembered. And then, quite suddenly, I was staring at a poem which did what all true, original poems do, left me gasping, knowing beyond doubt that I was in the presence of genius. The review I subsequently wrote for the *New Statesman*, inadequate though I'm sure it was, tried to alert readers to the fact that with the arrival of Kavanagh's edition the landscape of twentieth-century poetry had been permanently changed. I'm now even more certain than I was in 1982 that Gurney is one of the most original, extraordinary, and *essential* of twentieth-century poets. The pages that follow are an attempt to offer some sort of justice to a poet it feels small-minded not to call great.

Biographical Outline

1890   Ivor Bertie Gurney born 28 August, 3 Queen Street, Gloucester, second of four children born to David Gurney, tailor, and Florence (née Lugg). A few years later the family will move to 19 Barton Street, to a house and shop combined.

1896   Purchase of family piano.

1899   Joins choir of All Saints Church.

1900   Wins place at Gloucester Cathedral Choir and King's School. Keen footballer, at which game he shows great skill and competitive instinct.

1904   Sings at Three Choirs Festival. Begins to compose music.

1905   Begins close association with Revd Alfred Hunter Cheesman, who acted as godfather at his christening, and with the sisters Margaret and Emily Hunt, all of whom encourage his musical talents.

1906   Articled pupil of Dr Herbert Brewer, organist of Gloucester Cathedral. Has temporary posts as organist at Whitminster, Hempsted and the Mariner's Church, Gloucester. Becomes friends with Herbert Howells, F. W. Harvey, a local poet, and John Haines, the solicitor and acquaintance of many writers.

1907   Passes matriculation examination at Durham University, but takes the matter no further.

1911   Wins scholarship to the Royal College of Music of £40 per annum. Cheesman provides a further £40. Takes digs in Fulham. As a student at the College Gurney becomes friendly with Marion Scott and Ethel Voynich. Is taught composition by Charles Stanford and comes under the musical influence of Ralph Vaughan

	Williams. Perhaps also through Williams's influence he discovers the poetry of Walt Whitman.
1913	Begins to write verse. Suffers from nervous problems diagnosed as 'Neurasthenia' and recuperates at Framilode and Gloucester.
1914	On 4 August, war is declared against Germany. Gurney volunteers for the army but is rejected. Restless, he abandons his studies and takes post as organist at Christ Church, High Wycombe, where he makes the acquaintance of the Chapman family.
1915	9 February, joins 5th Gloucester Reserve Battalion, the 2nd/5th Glosters. The battalion goes to Northampton and then, in April, to Chelmsford. In June the battalion goes to Epping, from where Gurney sends Marion Scott the first poem that will appear in *Severn & Somme*. By August the battalion is back in Chelmsford.
1916	After further moves – including Tidworth – the battalion finally crosses to France, arriving at Le Havre on 25 May. For the next year and a half, until September 1917, Gurney is in France, experiencing front-line action at various places, including Riez Bailleul, Richebourg-St Vaast, Aubers Bridge, Albert, Vermand, Guemappe, Ypres, and St Julien. During this time he becomes his platoon's crack shot. For fuller details of Gurney's time in France see the 'Chronology' supplied by George Walter to his edition of *Rewards of Wonder* (MidNAG/Carcanet, 2000, pp. 146–58).
1917	7 April, wounded in upper arm. 14 July, Sidgwick & Jackson agree to publish a collection of Gurney's. 10 September, gassed at St Julien. While in hospital, corrects proofs of *Severn & Somme*. Then, 22 September, put on board ship for England and three days later is in Edinburgh War Hospital, where he meets and falls in love with Annie Drummond, a VAD nurse. In November he is granted leave, the same month is transferred to Seaton Delaval for a signalling course (in the hope he will be fit enough to return to active duty), and on the 16th *Severn & Somme* is published.
1918	12–18 February, visits his father, who has cancer. Is examined for effects of gas and admitted to Newcastle

General Hospital. A month later he tells Marion Scott he has spoken to the 'spirit of Beethoven'. In May, deeply disturbed, he is sent to Lord Derby's War Hospital, Warrington, a hospital which pioneered the use of electrical charges in dealing with shell-shock, although there's no evidence it was tried on Gurney. A month later, 19 June, he sends Marion Scott a suicide note. On 4 October he is discharged from the army. Works in a munitions factory and makes several attempts to go to sea. 11 November, on declaration of Armistice, ceases work at the factory.

1919   Returns to Royal College of Music but soon moves back to Gloucester. In May his second collection of poems, *War's Embers*, is published. On 10th of that month his father dies. Moves from place to place, job to job, and in October experiences some sort of mental crisis.

1920   More of the same. In May tries to set up home in rural Gloucestershire, by October is back in London, living in lodgings in Earl's Court. Writes and composes much.

1921   Again, peripatetic. In July, finally leaves the Royal College of Music. Two poems published in J. C. Squire's *Selections From Modern Poets*. Winthrop Rogers publish *Five Preludes For Piano*. Throughout the year, various jobs, as farm worker in Gloucestershire, cold storage worker in London, cinema pianist in Bude.

1922   Sidwick & Jackson twice reject a collection of poems. Work on farm, in Gloucester Tax Office, then, in September, tries to commit suicide. On 28 September is certified insane and admitted to Barnwood House, a private asylum in Gloucester. Escapes on two separate occasions and on 21 December is transferred to the City of London Mental Hospital at Dartford, where he will spend the rest of his life.

1923   Poems in the *London Mercury* and *The Listener*. Stainer & Bell publish *Five Western Watercolours* and *Ludlow and Teme* as part of the Carnegie Collections of British Music. Early in January Gurney escapes from hospital and goes to London to see J. C. Squire and Vaughan Williams. Perhaps as a result of this, the latter wishes to have a collection of Gurney's poems made for him.

1924   Writes both poetry and music and has poems published

	in the *London Mercury*. Announces he has seven manuscript books of poetry ready for typing, including the one now known as *Rewards of Wonder*.
1925	Writes *The Book of Five Makings* and, during the course of the year, many other poems as well as songs and instrumental music.
1926–7	Writes and has published songs and poems.
1928	February, Gollancz consider publishing a collection of Gurney's poems, though nothing comes of it. Some of his songs published by Oxford University Press.
1929–31	Still writing and, occasionally, publishing music and poetry.
1932	Visited by Helen Thomas, who brings with her Edward Thomas's O.S. maps of Gloucestershire.
1933–4	Poems published in the *London Mercury*. (Four in 1933, twelve in 1934.)
1935–7	Gerald Finzi and Marion Scott plan for the publication of a symposium on Gurney's work in *Music and Letters*. Walter de la Mare agrees to write the introduction for an edition of Gurney's poems. Gurney's health is deteriorating fast and in November 1937 he is diagnosed as suffering from pleurisy and tuberculosis. 26 December, dies from bilateral pulmonary tuberculosis. 31 December, buried at Twigworth, Gloucestershire. Service conducted by Canon Cheesman.
1938	*Music and Letters* carries the Symposium on his work. Oxford University Press publish two volumes of his songs.

Abbreviations

Everyman   *Ivor Gurney*, ed. George Walter (London: Dent/ Everyman, 1996)

Kavanagh   *Collected Poems of Ivor Gurney*, ed. P. J. Kavanagh (Oxford: Oxford University Press, 1982)

Letters   *Ivor Gurney: Collected Letters*, ed. R. K. R. Thornton (Ashington, Northumberland: MidNAG; Manchester: Carcanet, 1991)

1

Becoming a Poet

First, some facts. Ivor Gurney was born in Gloucester on 28 August 1890, the second of four children. His sister Winifred had been born in 1886, Ronald followed in 1894, and Dorothy six years later. Their father, David Gurney, was a tailor who ran his own shop, and his wife, born Florence Lugg, and older than her husband by five years, who was also trained in tailoring, helped with needle and thread when domestic chores allowed. According to Michael Hurd, 'David Gurney was a Severn Valley man, from the low-lying fields around Maisemore. Florence Lugg came from Bisley, high in the hills above Stroud. He was gentle, placid, ruminative. Her temperament was much chillier, and given to anxious storms.'

Hurd goes on to remark that in 1896 the Gurneys, who seem to have enjoyed music, bought a pianoforte, 'a sign of increasing respectability'. But many working-class families owned pianos. They weren't so much signs of respectability as evidence of people's ability to find pleasure and entertainment through music. All the Gurney children were given music lessons. This, too, was common enough. And still more commonly they heard and enjoyed the music provided in their local church. For the Gurneys this was All Saints, where Ivor Gurney was soon to become one of the curate's, Alfred Cheesman's, 'boys'. Cheesman was, so Hurd suggests, homoerotic rather than homosexual, an adherent of what Paul Fussell has called in his chapter on 'Soldier Boys' in *The Great War and Modern Memory*, 'mutual affection, protection, and admiration'. This was after all the period of that 'Uranianism' which can be in large measure traced to Oxford, of which Cheesman was a graduate. And Uranianism was characterized, again to use Fussell's words, by 'the attractions and usually the impeccable morality of boy love'.[1] The friendship with Cheesman lasted into Gurney's adulthood. Indeed, Cheesman was to officiate at Gurney's funeral. And for all that Gurney may be accounted one of the awkward squad, he never lacked for friends of both sexes. In 1900 he won a place in the Gloucester Cathedral choir and at King's School. A few years later, when he began to write music, he was encouraged not merely by Cheesman but by Emily Hunt. Fifteen years older than Gurney, she was one of two sisters, a violinist and woman of modest but independent means, who met Gurney through Cheesman's good offices. Soon afterwards he was to form close and lasting friendships with Herbert Howells, F. W. Harvey, (the 'Gloucestershire poet'), and a local solicitor, John Haines, who knew many writers of both regional and national significance, and who seems to have meant as much to Gurney as Edward Marsh meant to the Georgian poets, above all Rupert Brooke. (Although Brooke meant far more to Marsh.)

In 1911 Gurney won a scholarship to the Royal College of Music. Further friendships now developed, perhaps the most crucial being with Marion Scott. Like Emily Hunt, Scott was an older woman – she had been born in 1877 – who had studied at the Royal College, and was among other things a music critic. She soon became devoted to Gurney. Howells joined Gurney at the College, and the pair made friends with Arthur Benjamin. But Scott's friendship was extra-special. It was she who looked after the drafts of Gurney's poems which he began to send her almost as soon as he began to write verse. Whatever criticisms can be levelled at Scott – and she wasn't an especially acute critic of his work – she provided invaluable support during his difficult, tormented life. Moreover, she looked after his letters and, more important, poems, did her best to arrange for publication of collections of his work, and in general behaved with forbearance and genuine disinterestedness towards someone she knew was a genius. Nobody who cares about Gurney can be other than eternally grateful to her.

His first poems seem to belong to 1912, though it's difficult to know whether he took them seriously. It's not unusual for young men and women to want to write verse, and Gurney was moving in a milieu where an interest in the arts was taken for granted. Moreover, he knew Harvey, he read older contemporary poets such as Housman and Yeats, he visited Harold Monro's Poetry Bookshop, which had opened at the tail end of 1912, and through which he came to know of Marsh's stable of Georgian poets; and two years later, in the early summer of 1914 he was made aware, through Haines, of the 'Dymock Poets', Wilfred Gibson, Lascelles Ambercrombie and the others. I've no reason to suppose he had read all their work, but he certainly knew and approved of Abercrombie's, and his letters make abundantly clear that he was always an enthusiastic admirer of Gibson.

By the time these poets set up home in the small village on the Gloucestershire–Herefordshire border, Gurney had recovered from the nervous depression – 'neurasthenia' was the diagnosis – which had knocked him off balance in the previous year. He was now writing a good deal of verse and showing the results to friends. Yet I suspect he continued to think of himself as more committed to music than to poetry. Certainly a letter of early 1914 to his great friend, Harvey, bursts with the joy of someone who has discovered in himself the gift of composition.

> Willy, Willy. I have done five of the most delightful and beautiful songs you ever cast your beaming eyes upon. They are all Elizabethan – the words – and blister my kidneys, bisurate my magnesia if the music is not as English, as joyful, as tender as any of all that noble host. Technique all right, and as to word setting – models. 'Orpheus', 'Tears', 'Under the Greenwood Tree', 'Sleep' and 'Spring'. How did such an undigested clod as I make them? That, Willy, I cannot say. But there they are – 'Five Songs' for Mezzo Soprano – 2 flutes, 2 clarinets, a harp and two bassoons.
>
> By Ivor Gurney A.R.C.O.
>
> Yes, Willy, I got through that exam and meningite my cerebralis if I didn't get Second Prize! (*Letters*, p. 10).

II

A few months later, on 4 August 1914, war was declared. Gurney immediately volunteered, was refused, but early next year joined the 5th Gloucester Reserve Battalion, the '2nd/5th Glosters'. It is now that he begins to write poetry seriously.

One reason for this is obvious enough. Soldiers deprived of musical instruments could easily get hold of pencil and paper. Another is that some men knew deep in their bones that the events of August 1914 opened a momentous, even definitive, moment in world history. There was therefore a felt need to try to be adequate to the moment: to have your say, to leave your mark. Hence, those hundreds upon hundreds of mostly pathetically and hopelessly bad volumes of schoolboy verse which crowded the bookstalls during the war years. Third, the death of Rupert Brooke in April 1915 undoubtedly acted as trigger for other would-be soldier-poets to declare themselves. Gurney's first collection, *Severn & Somme*, concludes with five 'Sonnets 1917', dedicated 'To the Memory of Rupert Brooke'. Two years earlier, in April 1915, Gibson had similarly dedicated his collection, *Friends*, 'To The Memory Of Rupert Brooke' and *Friends* opened with four sonnets to Brooke. In between 1915 and 1917 came more such dedications.

We might therefore imagine *Severn & Somme* to be a conventional enough collection of war poetry. And so it mostly is. For all that Gurney had discovered Whitman in the autumn on 1915 – 'he has taken me like a flood' he wrote to a woman friend – there's little evidence of the American poet's influence on Gurney's early poetry. The collection is on the whole made up of conventional exercises, both technically and in what the poems say about the war. Most of them were written in France, where the Glosters were sent in May 1916. From there, Gurney posted poems back to Marion Scott. In October 1916 he told her that he wanted to write more poems 'chiefly of local interest, make a book and call it *Songs from the Second-Fifth*'. By 'local interest' Gurney means Gloucestershire. Marion Scott approached the publishers, Sidgwick & Jackson, showed them such poems as she had, and they agreed to take the collection.

Michael Hurd tells us that Sidgwick & Jackson had already published Harvey's *A Gloucestershire Lad* 'with considerable success'. This is so, but we need to add that by then the firm had become one of the leading publishers for volumes of war poetry, all of which did well. I have on my own shelves Katherine Tynan's popular *Flower of Youth: Poems in War Time*, which Sidgwick & Jackson first published in 1915. It includes a poem called 'The Great Chance', about a black sheep of a family who comes good by volunteering for action and getting himself killed. The last stanza runs:

> They [the black sheep's parents] tell, with proud and stricken face
>> Of his white boyhood far away –
> Who talked of trouble or disgrace?
>> 'Our splendid son is dead!' they say.

I also possess Jeffrey Day's *Poems and Rhymes* (1919), the verses of an airman killed in action. A Memoir at the head of this little collection ends as follows:

> His service, done in the spirit in which he did it, requires more valour and endurance than have ever been required of man before. He met the new call and did more than meet it: he thrust ahead and with his poet's fire lit a new beacon on the path of duty. The memory of him and his fellow-knights will be the treasure of all English hearts in after time. We bear it in trust for them.

Although Day was no poet, I don't quote these words to mock either him or them. But the language of chivalry on which the Memoir haplessly depends – of valour and knights – is significant. For this was how the war was so often and so betrayingly regarded, especially in its early years: knights in armour engaged in honourable fight. This is at the heart of one of the most popular of all collections of war poetry put out by Sidgwick & Jackson, Herbert Asquith's *The Volunteer and Other Poems*. Like *Flower of Youth*, Asquith's much reprinted volume was first published in 1915. In other words its innocent belief in a 'good war' pre-dates the growing disillusionment, cynicism, bitter anger and despair, which come to be the defining characteristics of poetry written in the war's later years. By then, and especially after the horror of the Somme and, still more, Passchendaele, there was widespread contempt among soldiers for the incompetence of generals, the self-serving hypocrisy of politicians, and, perhaps most of all, a deep hatred for armaments manufacturers and newspaper proprietors, those bogus patriots who spoke of the Holy Cause for which others would gladly pay the 'supreme sacrifice' while they got on with the essential work of stuffing their pockets. And the longer war went on, the better war-profiteers liked it.

Needless to say, that wasn't how matters looked in 1915. War was then still idealized as a great adventure. Herbert Asquith's

5

volunteer is, not untypically we may feel, a clerk who gladly exchanges the grey routines of a desk-bound job in the city for the chance to break 'a lance in life's tournament'. And in a companion poem, 'The Western Line', the dead soldiers of rival armies are seen in terms that suggest a school rugger match. 'The floods of battle ebb and flow/The soldiers to Valhalla go... //To banquet with their foes.'

There's a good deal of this in *Severn & Somme*. Something, too, of Brooke's delight and anticipation of war as providing the opportunity to turn from a world 'grown old and cold and weary'. So Gurney's 'Acquiescence' celebrates the boy-soldier who embraces battle 'Before the smut of the world and the lust of money,/Power and fame, can yet his youth destroy'. Better the quick, 'clean' death in battle than the lingering death-in-life of modern existence. And in echo of Julian Grenfell's 'Into Battle', with its exultant belief in war as physical release, Gurney writes, in 'Scots', of a charge 'Over the top this morning at the first flush of day'. In addition, and in common with others who rushed into print during the war, Gurney offers his tribute

> To England's royal grace and dignity,
> To England's changing skies, rich greenery,
> High strength controlled, queenly serenity,
> Inviolate kept by her confederate sea
> And hearts resolved to every sacrifice.
> We shall come home again...
> The last farthing paid of the Great Cost,
> The last thrill suffered of the Great Pain.

While 'Spring, Rouen, May 1917' isn't as bad as 'England the Mother', the sonnet which ends the collection, I can well imagine that these lines, quoted out of context and set beside others already quoted, might be enough to cause anyone to wonder what all the fuss is about.

But we need to remember that at the outset of the war the cause seemed to most Englishmen and women a just one. Leave the hysteria of the 'Hun-hating' British press out of it. The fact remains that Germany was the chief aggressor. This doesn't, however, mean that those who enlisted or encouraged war always or unambiguously exonerated England from blame. England seemed to surfeit on its own excess of wealth. Although the most obvious symbol of that excess, Edward VII, had died four years earlier, England in 1914 was nevertheless a nation where the inequalities of rich and poor were vast and where the celebration of ostentatious riches sickened many. Hence, the Dymock experiment. Hence, those many utopian socialist communes which established themselves in the Cotswolds, and about which there will be more to say later. Hence, the rise of various forms of radical politics, Suffragettism, Fabianism, the ILP (Independent Labour Party), Anarchism – which, whatever their differences, had in common a profound detestation of 'the smut of the world and the lust of money'.

Besides, going into battle undoubtedly appealed to many young men who imagined the war would be a cavalry war, as, for example, Grenfell believed: swift-moving, providing opportunities for acts of individual courage and chivalric behaviour, and, best of all, soon over. I don't say all these reasons for rejoicing at the chance to fight sit easily together. Nor do they all make sense, and certainly not from a later vantage point. But there's no reason to doubt the sincerity of those thousands upon thousands of young men who in the early months of the war eagerly committed themselves to what was at the time habitually spoken of as 'the great adventure'. It was only as the war went on and the murderous incompetence of Haig and his fellow generals became evident that the initial ardour cooled; and when it became equally evident that war was being prolonged to suit 'the bosses', then cynicism, despair, or the altogether more useful anger replaced earlier idealism. Most of the poems that make up *Severn & Somme* belong to what we might call an innocent response to the war. In this, they are no better nor worse than other such collections put out by Sidgwick & Jackson and other publishers during the years 1914–18.

Yet against this we can set poems of Gurney's which refuse to act the innocent. Take 'To England – a Note'.

> I watched the boys of England where they went
> Through mud and water to do appointed things.
> See one a stake, and one wire-netting brings,
> And one comes slowly under a burden bent
> Of ammunition. Though the strength be spent
> They 'carry on' under the shadowing wings
> Of Death the ever-present. And hark, one sings
> Although no joy from the grey skies be lent.

Are these the heroes – these? have kept from you
The power of primal savagery so long?
Shall break the devil's legions? These they are
Who do in silence what they might boast to do;
In the height of battle tell the world in song
How they do hate and fear the face of War.

Easy enough to pick holes in this, and it's to be wished that someone *had* picked holes in it before it saw the light of day. But that someone would have to have been Marion Scott who, as I have already noted, lacked the critical skills to help Gurney. Indeed, it seems proper to remark that Gurney never enjoyed the kind of affectionate, rigorous relationship with a fellow writer which, for example, was so important to the friendship of Edward Thomas and Robert Frost. This makes his ultimate achievement all the more astonishing; but it also means that he had to find his own way. As a result, he took some time to get rid of the awkward amateurism, the padding, the duff syntactic inversion – and all for the sake of a poor rhyme – that between them sink the line 'Although no joy from the grey skies be lent'. On the other hand, the carry over of 'under a burden bent/Of Ammunition', gauche though it is here, hints at a tactical device Gurney learns to put to entirely effective use in his mature, great work.

It is, however, the ending of this sonnet which most matters, because for the first time we catch Gurney turning away from convention, hear a more truly radical voice emerging out of the pieties and unconsidered clichés of most war poetry. Gurney says that 'the boys' – and in poems to come he'll make repeated use of that term – 'In the height of battle tell the world in song/ How they do hate and fear the face of War'. The shock of the last line in large measure depends on Gurney setting up 'song' as anticipation of the lyric utterance of patriotic sentiment or insouciant revelry to be expected of 'boys' in war. This was after all how the boys were supposed to sing. Not in this poem, however. *This* song turns out to be one of protest or unheroic fear. In the helpful notes to his edition of *Severn & Somme and War's Embers* (1997), Kelsey Thornton refers to a letter to Marion Scott of 22 June 1916, in which Gurney writes out both tune and words of 'The Song that Signallers Sung and Stretcher bearers of C company, when the great guns roared at them, and the Germans thought to attack'.

I want to go home, I want to go home,
The whizz bangs and shrapnel they rattle and roar:
I don't want to go on the top any more
Take me over the sea,
Where the allemans can't catch me
O my I don't want to die
I want to go home.

The songs the soldiers sang in the trenches of the Great War is of course a notable feature of *vox pop*. 'The Bells of Hell', 'I Don't Want to Join the Army', 'We're Here Because We're Here', and the one Gurney sets down for Marion Scott: these and many others, scabrous, bawdy, irreverent, *funny*, all share an attitude to war far removed from Officialdom's account of that attitude: heroic, uncomplaining, joyously patriotic. Gurney, who was well aware of the revival of interest in folk-song that had for some years been under way by the time he arrived at the Royal College of Music, was presented in the trenches with folk-song in the making.

But there's more to it than that. Just how much more can be seen if we link 'To England – a Note' with other poems in *Severn & Somme*. The triolet 'Strafe', for example, announces 'The "crumps" are falling twenty to the minute./We crouch and wait the end of it or us', and contrasts the barbarous noise of high explosive with '(Framilode! O Maisemore's laughing linnet.)' That line apart, the triolet is one of wry fatalism, and the invocation of loved places in Gloucestershire, held within brackets, emphasizes their remoteness from war-time France. The triolet belongs recognizably within the same web of feeling that catches Bruce Bairnfather's famous 'Old Bill', the archetypal 'Tommy' who, in one of Bairnfather's most widely circulated cartoons, stares with amused contempt at the nervous, younger soldier with whom he shares a shell-hole while 'whizz-bangs' burst all around. 'Well,' he says, 'if you know of a better 'ole, go to it.'

But wry fatalism is by no means the only, or even dominant, tone of *Severn & Somme*. The volume ends with a sequence of five sonnets called 'Sonnets 1917', and dedicated 'To the Memory of Rupert Brooke'. The sequence may seem to be meant as both homage and imitation, homage *because* imitation. For Brooke's sonnet sequence called, '1914', had also been made up of five sonnets, and Gurney follows the Petrarchan form which Brooke had adopted for his sonnets. But it soon becomes clear that Gurney is not so much acknowledging as challenging the propriety of Brooke's attitude to war. And so, in the second sonnet called 'Pain', Gurney writes:

> Pain, pain continual; pain unending;
> Hard even to the roughest, but to those
> Hungry for beauty....Not the wisest knows
> Nor most-pitiful hearted, what the wending
> Of one hour's way meant.

The sonnet ends:

> Men broken, shrieking even to hear a gun. –
> Till pain grinds down, or lethargy numbs her,
> The amazed heart cries angrily out on God.

Why God, we may wonder? Why not High Command? But to ask the question is to anticipate the answer. Not only would crying angrily at Haig amount to sedition, it would ensure that Sidgwick & Jackson knocked out the poem and perhaps even cancelled the whole volume. Still, even as it stands, we may be surprised that the poem got through. But then 'Pain' is the second sonnet. By the time we get to the fifth and final one – 'England and Mother' – we're back on safe ground. This sonnet's closing sestet runs:

> Thy love, thy love shall cherish, make us whole,
> Whereto the power of Death's destruction is weak.
> Death impotent, by boys bemocked at, who
> Will leave unblotted in the soldier-soul
> Gold of the daffodil, the sunset streak,
> The innocence and joy of England's blue.

Rupert Brooke can rest easy after all.

Or can he? For that Gurney hardly believed this stuff is evident not merely from the tushery of 'Thy love, thy love', but from the perfunctory clichés which are wheeled out to identify pastoral England. This is 'poetry' going through the motions, and although it may be that Gurney *did* try to persuade himself that he felt about the war as Brooke had done, the sonnet's routine language and sentiments, just because they are *so* uninspected, suggest his heart, and, more important, head, weren't in it. Moreover, a glance at his letters alerts us to the fact that he wasn't really at ease with Brooke's sonnets. He didn't *believe* them. From time to time he lists Brooke as one of the important poets of the war, which in a sense he was. No other poet was so widely quoted, nor had his poems more often reprinted. Yet from the first Gurney is sceptical of Brooke's achievement. As early as August 1915, thanking Marion Scott for the gift of one of Brooke's sonnets, he says he doesn't much like it. 'Brooke would not have improved with age,' he tells her, 'his manner has become a mannerism.... Great poets, great creators are not much influenced by immediate events; these must sink in to the very foundations and be absorbed. Rupert Brooke soaked it in quickly and gave it out with as great ease' (*Letters*, 29). Gurney's recognition that Brooke was trading in superficial attitudes to war, that his invocations to England and glory were equally superficial, 'easy' in the sense that they didn't proceed from hard thought – this is surely both spot on and, given its date, daring in its iconoclasm.

But a pair of later letters to Scott, written in February 1917, and enclosing two of the sonnets, best explain Gurney's position. In the first, dated 7 February, in which he encloses a copy of 'Pain', he tells her that his sonnets are 'for admirers of Rupert Brooke. They will make good antitheses', though he reassures her that 'Pain' is 'the blackest' of the sequence. A week later, he returns to the subject. 'These Sonnetts ... are intended to be a sort of counterblast against "Sonnetts 1914", which were written before the grind of war and by an officer (or one who would have been an officer.) They are the protest of the physical against the exalted spiritual; of the cumulative weight of small facts against one large. Of informed opinion against uninformed (to put it coarsely and unfairly) and fill a place. Old ladies won't like them, but soldiers may...' (*Letters*, 203, 210). By soldiers Gurney means Tommy Atkins, the ordinary line soldiers with whom he mixed, whose songs, jokes, and, as he said in a great poem, 'infinite lovely chatter' he relished. It was for and about *them* he was writing.

The importance of this decision can hardly be overestimated. Earlier war poetry, and some that went on being written until war's end, was all-too plainly produced in order to confirm that the writer was at one with patriotic feeling and determined to

11

defeat the enemy while having a good time playing the game of war. I don't say such poetry was cynical in its intention. It most certainly wasn't. (Although it could be, and was, cynically exploited by war-mongers.) But as the war became bloodier, more terribly destructive, its motives increasingly questionable, producing poetry which uncritically echoed the Brooke Position became, for real poets at least, what Wilfred Owen memorably called 'the old lie'. He and his poet-friend, Siegfried Sassoon, who in the early days of the war wrote entirely conventional Brooke-alike poems, developed and changed as the war dragged on. They, too, began writing for their fellow soldiers and in radical defiance of the weight of conventional support for the war – support which was inevitably the more absolute the further people were from the war itself. So it was for Gurney. And even if not all his poems were about his fellow soldiers, it seems proper to say that they were for them.

Whether they liked the poems I've no idea. *Severn & Somme* sold well, although the size of its print-run isn't known; and anyway, its comparative financial success is no guarantee of quality. Many far worse collections sold a great deal better. They always do. But who could fail to recognize the rare quality of the following?

> Only the wanderer
> > Knows England's graces,
> Or can anew see clear
> > Familiar faces.
>
> And who loves joy as he
> > That dwells in shadows?
> Do not forget me quite,
> > O Severn meadows.

'How did such an undigested clod as I make them?' Genius, I suppose. From time to time Gurney will produce other miraculously beautiful little lyrics, but I don't know that he made any to equal this unimprovable song, its rythmic pulse answering to song-like cadence rather than the alternate three- and two-stress lines into which it formally breaks, the soon-to-be characteristic feminine rhyming pattern also more usually found in song than in poetry intended for the page. In his review of the volume for the *Morning Post*, E. B. Osborne shrewdly noted how the musician in Gurney comes out 'in the subtle avoidance of all jog-trot, this-way-to-the-market, rhythms, and in the artistic management of vowel-sounds, and in the use of the diminished double-rhyme (honour...manner...- praises...

faces, and so on) all of which give his verse an air of distinction even when he had no time to polish it'.[2]

That's well said. I'd want to add only that as far as 'Song' is concerned, the drama of the poem is partly dependent on the turn from the generalized 'he' to 'me', and that this is further intensified by the little word 'quite', with its plea for the merest glimmer of a presence among the Severn meadows. And I'd note, too, how the invocation that opens the last line and the line's linked vowel sounds O, picked up in the poem's final vowel, but held in suspension by the assonance of the first syllables of *Sev*ern and *Mead*ows, adds to the ache for ultimate harmony, ultimate return.

'Song' is in some ways a ghost poem, almost Hardyesque in its sense of the wanderer as invisible presence, the dweller in shadows revisiting loved ground. Not far away from 'shadows' is 'shades', with its appeal to that classical idea of the place reserved for the dead. Gurney doesn't go so far as to say that his spirit will hover among the Severn meadows to which he felt himself so intensely to belong, but his plea 'Do not forget me quite', at once urgent and tentative, tells of his desire to (re)locate himself in that native place, to be *present* there. (I use 'present' in the sense identified by the *OED* with presence: 'A Being beside, with, or in the same place as the person who or thing which is the point of reference; being in the place in question'.) Imagining the likelihood of death's shadow closing over him, as which soldier did not, Gurney yearns to be in some sense re-united with or returned to what's familiar, known and loved.

Death's shadow is also present in 'Ballad of the Three Spectres', the poem which follows 'Song'. In this strange, compelling poem, its narrative strategy certainly derived from 'The Twa Corbies', the great Scottish ballad Gurney knew and admired, he overhears as he marches to Ovillers three 'jeering, fleering spectres,/That walked abreast and talked of me'. The first says that Gurney will soon return on a stretcher, 'laughing for a nice Blighty'. Not so, the second replies. 'One day he'll freeze in mud to the marrow,/Then look his last on Picardie.'

13

And then the third spectre speaks. 'He'll stay untouched till the war's last dawning/Then live one hour of agony.' All soldiers must have brooded on those three alternatives: a blighty one (i.e. a wound which meant being invalided out of the army), death, or survival. But few would have thought the last alternative to entail living 'one hour of agony'. What had this to do with a hero's return?

Nothing, is the plain answer. On the other hand, it certainly fitted the case of those returning soldiers who found themselves without employment, physically and, still more disastrously, psychologically damaged by the war. An hour of agony was what awaited many thousands of those who survived trench warfare. In having the third spectre speak as he does, Gurney may well have had an inkling, a foreboding, of what the future would be for line soldiers. But he may also have been thinking of his own state of mind. If so, the third spectre was being prescient. So, as it happens, was the first spectre. On 7 April 1917, Gurney was wounded in the upper arm and spent some time out of the line. Then, on 10 September, he was gassed and invalided to the Edinburgh War Hospital, Bangour, where he met Annie Drummond, a VAD nurse, with whom he seems to have fallen in love, although the relationship didn't survive his transfer to Newcastle General Hospital in February 1918. He never returned to France or to active duties.

But nor had he obtained 'a nice Blighty'. Gurney's mental state now becomes precarious, a condition for which Annie Drummond certainly can't be held responsible. Whether war can, is more open to doubt. P. J. Kavanagh points out that Gurney's first mental collapse, in 1913, pre-dates the events of 1914–18; on the other hand, that breakdown was far less severe than the course his illness took in 1918. Hurd calls the illness of 1913 'a type of nervous breakdown brought on by the sustained effort of creative work'. Such breakdowns are not uncommon, especially among the gifted young. In 1918, however, he begins to suffer from hallucinations. On 28 March, he writes to Marion Scott that he has been visited by Beethoven, who 'said among other things that he was fond of me, and that in nature I was like himself as a young man ... What would the doctors say to that? A Ticket certainly, for insanity. No, it is the beginning of a new life, a new vision' (*Letters*, 418).

14

Worse is to come. On 19 June he sends Scott a note which he tells her 'is a good-bye letter, and written because I am afraid of slipping down and becoming a mere wreck – and I know you would rather know me dead than mad...' (*Letters*, 430). However, a letter of the following day says merely, 'Please forgive my letter of yesterday. I meant to do that I spoke of, but lost courage. Will you please let Sir Hubert know?' Sir Hubert Parry was one of Gurney's tutors at the Royal College, which Gurney was evidently planning to rejoin in order to complete his formal education. On 4 October he was discharged from the Army with a pension of twelve shillings a week. A full pension was denied him because his condition was judged to have been 'aggravated but not caused by' the war. A fine distinction it might seem to us, but however we view Gurney's discharge the fact is that in some sort he did survive the war. He also had a new volume of poems ready for publication.

III

War's Embers is a considerable advance on Gurney's first collection. The book is both technically more assured and intellectually more complex. In other words, more of Gurney has gone into it. This must in part be due to personal circumstances. Many of the poems were written, or anyway revised, after he'd been invalided out of France. Writing to Marion Scott about the poems that were to make up *Severn & Somme*, he confessed: 'You are right about the roughness of some of my work; there is no time to revise here, and if the first impulse will not carry the thing through, then what is written gets destroyed. One virtue I know little of – that is patience; and my mind is Hamlet's, a wavering self-distrustful me, though quick and powerful at its times. Will Peace bring me peace though' (*Letters*, 202). When he was preparing *War's Embers* he was, if far from being at peace, no longer at war.

In some respects the volume is, to be sure, still apprentice work. Gurney's reading of Yeats will account for his readiness to use the formulaic 'All's' ('All's a tangle', 'All's naught', 'All's equal'), just as 'The Fisherman of Newnham' is, no matter how unwittingly, a pastiche of 'The Fiddler of Dooney', a poem

15

Gurney greatly admired for its 'divine unliterate clearness'. (See *Letters*, 382–3.) And from Yeats he may well have borrowed the intensifier 'most', which becomes a stylistic tic in his own collection. ('Most fair', 'A green most kind', 'Most strangely fair', 'Most noble and complete', 'most friendly courteous', etc.).

He may, however, have picked this up from Edward Thomas. For Thomas, whose work Gurney was reading with increased avidity as he worked on the book, himself made use of the word on key occasions, as, for example, the 'owl's cry, a most melancholy cry', in a poem which Gurney held in especially high regard. Thomas is, in fact, a powerful presence in *War's Embers*. 'The Lock-Keeper', which is undoubtedly prompted by 'Lob', bears as epigraph 'To the Memory of Edward Thomas'. (Gurney later considerably expanded and improved the poem.) Thomas's example is in all likelihood behind Gurney's use of dialect speech in several poems, and it must affect poems where Gurney takes on a meditative pose which comes as near to Thomas's 'brooding' as he can manage, although Gurney habitually moves across lines with altogether greater rapidity, swifter lunges from image to image, idea to idea.

As for the sequence of six 'Hospital Pictures', they probably owe something to Gurney's attachment to Wilfrid Gibson's poetry. Gibson (1878–1962) was, at the time Gurney knew him, a poet with an international reputation, and Gurney greatly admired his work. Writing to Marion Scott of Gibson's *Friends*, a copy of which he bought and read soon after its publication in the spring of 1916, Gurney said that 'if anything could stir a lethargic brain, I think Gibson's little book would do it as well as anything... So clear a vision and so musical a speech must belong to physical and mental well-being. "I saw Three Pigs" is the very expression of spontaneous joy to be found in folksong and Bach preeminently' (*Letters*, 83). He was also struck, he told her, by poems of Gibson's which attempt to give utterance to a variety of voices, especially those of 'the common people'.

And here we begin to touch on a matter of utmost importance. In his poem 'On Rest', dedicated 'To the men of the 2/5 Gloucester Regiment', Gurney provides what seems a fairly unbuttoned account of soldiers relaxing out of line. All are together, united as a company in sharing the delights of 'First day on Rest, a Festival'.

16

Now wonders begin, Sergeants with the crowd
Mix; Corporals, Lance-Corporals, little proud,
Authority forgotten, all goes well
In this our Commonwealth, with tales to tell...
The Sergeant-major sheathes his claws and lies
Smoking at length, content deep in his eyes.
Officers like brothers chaff and smile –
Salutes forgotten, etiquette the while,
Comrades and brothers all, one friendly band.

The poem seems to have been written in July 1918, by which time Gurney was permanently invalided out of the army. He recalls a moment of holiday, of festival, of Commonwealth, when all men are truly comrades. Some years earlier he had discovered Whitman, that 'lover of common men' he told Marion Scott in a letter of 1916 (*Letters*, 130), a discovery which chimed with his delight in the 'Snatch of Shakespeare wit, from Pte. Tim Godding' (*Letters*, 70), and the talk of fellow Glosters. And we need then to note that his letters increasingly begin to doubt the justice of the war's continuation. His telling Scott in late July 1917 that although ready to die for England, 'I do not see the necessity; it being only a hard and fast system which has sent so much of the flower of England's artists to risk death, and a wrong materialistic system' (*Letters*, 288) may at a casual glance look like special pleading. But 'wrong materialistic system'. What can he mean by the phrase?

To answer that question we need to take note of remarks he lets drop in other letters to her, as when he writes in October 1916, 'The people here say that France was very happy and well governed before the war. Can you imagine an Englishman saying as much of England?' Some months later, in May 1917, he remarks that 'It is the bloomingest nuisance that a thing so well intended as the Russian Revolution can so upset things'. Kerensky's overthrow of the tsarist regime had led to considerable unrest in the Russian army and, sure enough, when Lenin overthrew Kerensky in October, Russia pulled out of the war. From letters he wrote during this period, it's clear that Gurney wanted to believe the Russian Army would remain committed to the Allied cause. But it's also clear that he welcomed the overthrow of the old regime. In August 1917, he is sure that we 'can look forward to great things', adding: 'I believe more in

Russia than you do'. And then, on 16 October, comes a crucial letter, when he tells her that

> It is of more importance that the Duke of Bilgewater should respect and sympathise with Bill Jones than that the sun should never set on the British Empire, whose liberties have been kept alive by revolt against the fathers of the present 'Prussians of England' (*Letters*, 353–4.)

He is in part replying to a letter of hers in which she had obviously taken fright at what is certainly an inflammatory sonnet enclosed with his previous letter.

TO THE PRUSSIANS OF ENGLAND

When I remember plain heroic strength
And shining virtue shown by Ypres pools,
Then read the blither written by knaves for fools
In praise of English soldiers lying at length,
Who purely dream what England shall be made
Gloriously new, free of the old stains
By us, who pay the price that must be paid,
Will freeze all winter over Ypres plains.
Our silly dreams of peace you put aside
And brotherhood of man, for you will see
An armed mistress, braggart of the tide,
Her children slaves, under your mastery.
We'll have a word there too, and forge a knife
Will cut the cancer threatens England's life.

Not surprisingly, the sonnet wasn't included in *War's Embers*. It does, after all, issue an unmistakable threat to those who wanted the war to go on, and who, in the process, deny the possibility of 'a brotherhood of man.' The poem could hardly have been written in response to the so-called October Revolution, because Lenin's assault on the Winter Palace occurred on 6–7 November; but he'd made an earlier attempt in July and the ten days that were to shake the world had been widely anticipated. There seems little doubt that Gurney, who with the Glosters had been forced to take part in the deadly absurdity of the battle of Passchendaele, which began on 31 July in mud and rain and was eventually to cost over half a million lives, had grown increasingly enraged by and contemptuous of those who were in charge of the war.

Nor was he alone in this. In a letter of 12 October 1917, he tells Marion Scott that 'the British soldier is absolutely confident of victory, and (since it must be) willing to go on. But O, what a hot time he will give some people after the war!' (*Letters*, 347). In 'To the Prussians of England', he is quite specific in referring to '*our* dreams of peace... and brotherhood of man'. And so, for all the relaxed tone of 'On Rest', we should note that, written as it was in July of the following year, and with the war coming to the close he had predicted (on 27 July 1917, with America about to join the Allied cause, he had told Marion Scott the war would end 'between July and September 1918'), the lines which rejoice that 'Authority forgotten, all goes well/In this our Common- wealth', look forward to *après la guerre* every bit as much as they look back to the actual occasion of a rest from line duties. In other words, the poem celebrates a socialistic commonwealth built out of the comings-together of men during the war. I've no doubt many of the men Gurney encountered in the trenches were already socialists. They would therefore have been included among those who, as he noted, 'if they return are to do the work and to shape England anew' (*Letters*, 129). He himself came in contact with socialist thought at the Royal College. Vaughan Williams, for example, was deeply sympa- thetic to socialist ideas. Moreover, Whitman, who 'has after some fashion renewed me', as Gurney told Marion Scott in 1916 (*Letters*, 128), was a poet of democratic vistas, one whose perfect man is 'equal to shepherd and President: equal and familiar' (*Letters*, 232). The men he writes about in 'On Rest' are 'Comrades and brothers all, one friendly band', where 'All's equal'. Such equality is very different from the England he had so angrily denounced to Marion Scott, when accounting for his poem 'To The Prussians of England'. This leads to a further point.

The lyric 'From Omiecourt', which Gurney seems to have written in late summer, 1918, begins 'Oh small dear things for which we fight'. These 'things' turn out to be part of his native Gloucestershire. 'Red roofs, ricks crowned with early gold,/ Orchards that hedges thick enfold'. In common with other poems written at this time, Gurney unashamedly identifies the cause for which he and others fight in terms of their native places. In 'Le Coq Français' he dreams of sleep that would bring a forgetting of all but 'home and old rambles, lovely days/Of maiden April, glamorous September haze,/All darling things of life'. In 'That County' he tells his reader 'Go up, go up your ways of varying love,/Take each his varying path wherever lie/The Central fires of secret memory'; and in 'De Profundis' he contrasts men in the trenches – they must be the Glosters – with their home county, and begs,

> O blow here, you dusk-airs and breaths of half-light,
>   And comfort despairs of your darlings that long
> Night and day for sound of your bells, or a sight
>   Of your tree-bordered lanes, land of blossom and song.

I doubt that any self-respecting poet would now risk introducing the word 'darling' into their work, except in the most controlled of contexts. Gurney, however, makes frequent, unironic use of it. He applies it to army comrades and to objects of his native place, and we need to be aware that its literal meaning was 'little dear.' The word's especial tenderness of address is therefore inseparable from Gurney's regard for 'small dear things'. And although in 'Camps', the poem from which the title *War's Embers* comes, he speaks grandly of 'The Pride/In sacrifice' of men who die 'for Freedom', 'Whose end was life abundant and increase' (an echo of Grenfell's 'And who dies fighting has increase') and who will thus find 'Heaven's gate wide opening [to receive] us/Victors and full of song, forgetting scars', these men are fighting for 'beauty/Of common living'.

This is crucial. What distinguishes Gurney from nearly all other soldier poets of the Great War is the ardour of his belief in what he will later call 'the dearness of common things'. By the time he wrote the poem which bears that title, sometime between 1920 and 1922, he had clearly come to appreciate Gerard Manley Hopkins's poetry far more than when first confronted with the poems Robert Bridges chose for his *Spirit of Man* (1915). 'Why all that... Hopkins or what's his names of the crazy precious diction?' he asked his correspondent, Mrs Voynich (*Letters*, 140). But with the publication in 1918 of something approaching a Complete Poems, Gurney changed his mind. For Hopkins, of course, the glory of dappled things belonged to God. Gurney merely gave thanks for the dearness of those common things he began to cherish as soon as he was away from them, in France. In a sense, he becomes their historian, rescuing them from oblivion, knowing their 'Hidden Tales', as the title of one poem in *War's Embers* has it. This poem, which speaks of plough horses uncovering 'The bones of many a lover/Unframed in tales;/Arrows, old flints of hammers', is not an especially good one. And Gurney's routine question, 'what splendid story/Lies here', and the equally routine dismissal 'None cares', manage to evade the fact that *he* plainly cares and that what he cares for is not so much splendour as ordinariness.

That the intensity of this care is strengthened by his being away from home, hardly needs saying. Nostalgia, this is usually called. The word is formed from two Greek words: 'Nostos' meaning home, and 'algos' pain. It was first coined in the late eighteenth century to account for the psychological hurt of Swiss Guards serving in foreign parts, and it has often enough modulated into an endorsement for wet-eyed regrets over a lost (usually mythic) past. But there is nothing sentimental about Gurney's attachment to the things of Gloucestershire and the Cotswolds. When, in 'Drifting Leaves', he recalls the 'trees that friended him', for example, he is doing no more than voice that sense of congruence, of fitting relationship, to be found elsewhere, as in Clare's great poem 'To a Fallen Elm' ('Old elm, that murmured in the chimney top'), and which William Barnes also speaks for in 'Trees be Company'. ('However lwonesome we mid be/The trees would still be company.')

Trees are common things, though the war made them less common. Millions were cut down to make gun carriages, munition carts, planks for trench duck-boards, and much else besides. Gurney, grieving over their loss, might well have mourned them as Hopkins mourned Binsey Poplars, lamenting their 'Beauty been'. For of all the words that stare uncompromisingly and defiantly out at us from the poems in *War's Embers*, the most challenging is undoubtedly that word 'beauty' or, as Gurney more often has it, 'Beauty'. As with 'darling', few poets would now risk using the word unless they hedged it round with irony. But early in the twentieth century the word is unembarrassedly introduced into poems by Yeats, for example, by Edward Thomas, and, especially, by Gurney. And it's therefore necessary to pin down the reasons for poets of that time making such habitual use of the word.

We know that Gurney read *Responsibilities* not long after it was published in 1914 and was stunned by the power of Yeats's great collection. In its pages he'd have encountered the poem 'To a Wealthy Man', with its evocation of Urbino's windy hill, 'Where wit and beauty learned their trade'. Yeats has in mind Castiglioni's *Book of the Courtier*, as is probably the case in an earlier poem, 'Adam's Curse', where a woman speaker is made to say that 'To be born woman is to know/Although they do not talk of it at school/That we must labour to be beautiful'. Yeats doesn't mean that girls should grow up wanting to win Miss World competitions. Here, and in his great elegy 'In Memory of Eva Gore-Booth and Con Markiewicz', where he recalls the two sisters, 'Both beautiful', the quality of which he speaks is a wholeness of being which is indifferent to worldly circumstance. Such beauty rests on its own inner certainty. It is non-utilitarian. It is also unlikely to thrive in the present, where people 'fumble in a greasy till'. For Yeats, 'Only the wasteful virtues earn the sun'. Indifference to prudential values is part of the beauty he extols. In a still earlier poem, 'He Remembers Forgotten Beauty', to be found in *The Wind among the Reeds*, (1899), Yeats places such beauty in a 'more dream-heavy land,/A more dream-heavy hour than this'. Such dreams hark back to a medieval spirit.

Behind Yeats is, as has been often enough remarked, the spirit of pre-Raphaelitism and, more important, perhaps, William Morris. Morris began as one of the PRB (Pre-Raphaelite Brotherhood), although by the time Yeats came to know him he had turned from dream to radical politics. Yeats couldn't follow him there, but he would have found much to agree with in Morris's persistent claims that 'the chief source of art is man's pleasure in his daily necessary work...nothing else can make the common surroundings of life beautiful, and whenever they are beautiful it is a sign that men's work has pleasure in it' ('The Worker's Share of Art'). Labouring to be beautiful is bound up with labouring to make beauty. In the same essay, Morris argues that leisure for working men breeds desire, 'desire for beauty, for knowledge, for more abundent life, in short'. Yeats would not have wanted to disagree with that, nor with the remark, in 'How We Live and How We Might Live', that 'beauty and fitness', which are to be desired for all, are best achieved through 'collective thought and collective life'. Yeats was after all a product of the Bedford Park community of artists and writers. At some deep level he would have assented to that vision in *News from Nowhere* in which Morris finds himself among 'beauty-loving people', opposed to the moral and spiritual ugliness of those who, before the change came, were 'Idleness stricken' because 'they used to force other people to work for them'.

This isn't to say that Yeats agreed with Morris's socialist concern for non-utilitarian beauty as desirable because achievable by and for all, for he very plainly didn't. But it is to say that he is at one with those who rejected those materialistic ways of living which, in every sense of the word, formed so ostentatious a phenomenon of pre-war England. And in this he'd have found something like common cause with such philosophers as George Santayana, whose *Sense of Beauty* was first published in 1896, and G. E. Moore, the author of *Principia Ethica*, 1903. I can't believe Moore was unaware of Santayana's treatise, although he makes no mention of it. But his claims for the intrinsic value of beauty are very close indeed to Santayana's argument that beauty as a value 'is enjoyed in and for itself ... without any thought of remote utility'. Moreover, 'The moral justification of art is in its creation of the beautiful. Whether that beauty be perfection of form, or an expression of other kinds of perfection, such as nobility of character, it is a partial realization of "the harmony between our nature and our experience ... a pledge of the possible conformity between the soul and nature ... a ground of faith in the supremacy of the good"'.[3]

For Moore, too, beauty, as he discusses it in his chapter, 'The Ideal', is an expression of the good. I should note in passing that Moore grants the beautiful may be a great many other things, and that he spends some time considering whether beautiful objects have essential characteristics. These arguments don't concern me. What does, is his assertion of the intrinsic value of beauty. In his study of Moore's philosophy, Thomas Baldwin quotes Bertrand Russell's enthusiastic endorsement of Moore's chapter on 'The Ideal', and comments, 'It is hard now to tell how striking Moore's commitment to the primacy of love and beauty appeared to his contemporaries'.[4] Not if you think of those contemporaries as including Edward Thomas and, a bit later, Gurney, it isn't.

Whether either poet read Santayana or Moore hardly matters.

In the ethos of resistance to that scrabbling for material wealth which was so marked a feature of both America and Britain at the turn of the century – it was what prompted Veblen's excoriating account of *Conspicuous Consumption* (1899), and, in England, Wells's *Tono Bungay* (1909) – the definition of Beauty as non-utilitarian becomes a key, one to be turned again and again as writers seek to unlock the doors of perception onto alternate ways of living. Hence, Thomas's 'Beauty', a poem which seems mired in the dark melancholy of spiritual and imaginative torpor, but which at the end lifts clear through a redemptive power 'That slants unswerving to its home and love./There I find my rest, and through the dusk air/Flies yet what lives in me. Beauty is there.'

'The Glory' begins in more ebullient mood, with 'The glory of the beauty of the morning'. But Thomas finds himself bound to earth, the glory leaving

> me scorning
> All I can ever do, all I can be,
> Beside the lovely of motion, shape, and hue,
> The happiness I fancy fit to dwell
> In beauty's presence. Shall I now this day
> Begin to seek as far as heaven, as hell,
> Wisdom or strength to match this beauty...
> And shall I ask at the day's end once more
> What beauty is, and what I can have meant
> By happiness?

In his persuasive account of this poem, Stan Smith remarks that 'Thomas lapses repeatedly from suspecting a real essence awaiting capture to reluctant acquiescence in a purely pragmatic notion of value'. This is undoubtedly so, and it may account for why, at the poem's conclusion, Thomas says, 'Beauty is there' rather than 'here'. Beauty as essence is always elusive.

But then to search for such essence, as 'Sedge-Warblers' suggests, is itself improperly utopian. 'This beauty made me dream there was a time/Long past and irrecoverable', the poem begins, but Thomas then confesses that 'rid of this dream, ere I had drained/Its poison, quieted was my desire/So that I only looked into the water...' Beauty may not be *there*, after all, but *here*, in the song of the sedge-warblers, 'Wisely reiterating endlessly/What no man learnt yet, in or out of school'.

If there is a discoverable, *proper* utopia, it has therefore to be in a future, imaginable England, whose roots are in the present. And this must surely be what Thomas has in mind when, in 'This is No Case of Petty Right or Wrong', he finds 'the storm smoking along the wind' to be 'Two witches' cauldrons.../From one the weather shall rise clear and gay;/Out of the other an England beautiful/And like her mother that died yesterday'. In other words, out of the cauldron of war will come a transformed England, yet one that is as England once was, not of course as it is in December 1915. The England with which Thomas identifies is a land of local pieties, of the dearness of common things. In the essay, 'It's a Long, Long Way', included in *The Last Sheaf*, Thomas writes:

> I should like to know what the old soldier meant by 'England'...His was a very little England. The core and vital principle was less still, a few thousand acres of corn, meadow, orchard, and copse, a few farms and cottages.

And in a companion essay, 'This England', in which he talks about why he decided to volunteer for active service, he says:

> Something, I felt, had to be done before I could look again composedly at English landscape, at the elms and poplars about the houses, at the purple-headed wood-betony with two pairs of leaves on a stiff stem, who stood sentinel among the grasses or bracken by hedge-side or wood's edge.

Beauty is in the particular.

So it is for Gurney. And for him, as for Thomas, the particular means the local. In a letter of 30 April 1917, he tells Marion Scott, 'Local poetry, local poetry is Salvation, and the more written the better' (*Letters*, 249). Admittedly, he is responding to Scott's gift of two copies of *Poetry Review*, a magazine, he says, 'devoted to the interests of weak but sincere verse'. But his intense regard for local things isn't qualified by irony. This is so obvious that it hardly needs to be set out in any detail, although Thomas is more *exactly* alert to local flora and fauna than Gurney. His 'brooding' goes with a kind of prolonged attentiveness which is very different from Gurney's 'rush'. (A word Gurney himself uses in his poem to Chapman and which sufficiently characterizes his own restless, impelled habits.)

But how inevitable it seems to link the two poets. And this is not merely because they both have connections with the Cotswolds, nor because their concern for values they cherish has nothing essential in it of patriotic grandeur, but because they are at one identifying beauty, or, in Gurney's case, Beauty, as a value that can be set against the utilitarian. In this context, therefore, we must note how often Gurney reaches for the word in his invocations to or descriptions of music, that least referential of the arts. Here, for example, is the sonnet, 'After Music', which Thornton says was written in October 1917, and 'was the first poem Gurney wrote since returning to Britain suffering from the effects of gas'. He enclosed it in a letter sent to Marion Scott on 8 October.

> Why, I am on fire, and tremulous
>> With sense of Beauty long denied; the first
>> Opening of the floodgate to the glorious burst
> Of freedom from the Fate that limits us
> To work in darkness pining for the light,
>> Thirsting for sweet untainted draughts of air,
>> Clouds sunset coloured, Music...O Music's bare
> White heat of silver passion fiercely bright!
> While sweating at the foul task, we can taste
>> No Joy that's clean, no Love but something lets
>> It from its power; the wisest soul forgets
> What's beautiful, or delicate, or chaste.
> Orpheus drew me (as once his bride) from Hell.
> If wisely, her or me, the Gods can tell.

'After Music' belongs to the same moment as 'To the Prussians of England'. Music, Gurney says, is that embodiment of Joy rinsed clear ('untainted', 'clean') of the foulness of war. In a letter to Marion Scott dated 16 October – the very same day he wrote to her, in another letter, about the Duke of Bilgewater – Gurney tells her that the last line of the sonnet 'is meant to be quizzical. *Is* it wise for me to play music? Well, I do, but know only too well that the effort to forget will be an extra difficulty against the little serenity I shall have in France' (*Letters*, 350). He's clearly anticipating that, once recovered, he'll be ordered back to the trenches. In the event, that wasn't to happen, but 'After Music' reveals that the 'foul task' of war, where men are probably best off forgetting a world of Beauty, is one that condemns them to 'work in darkness, pining for the light'. In the Book of *Job*, God is said to make people 'grope in the darkness without light', and this cursed state was often used in the nineteenth century to suggest the plight of working men and women. In Edwin Arlington Robinson's 'Richard Cory' (1897), the people of the pavement glumly speak of how 'we worked, and waited for the light,/And went without the meat, and cursed the bread'. Richard Cory seems to them an image of almost Gatsby-like ethereal beauty, far above their humdrum lives. Robinson's sardonic, protestant imagination won't allow him to identify with Cory. But Gurney's rapt identification with music has surely to be set *against* the horrors of war as well as *with* his growing sense that those who fight are, as he says in a letter already quoted, doing so for 'a wrong materialistic system'. And that letter, we should note, was written no more than two months before 'After Music'.

Knowing this, we can the better understand why, in the sixth, last and best of the Hospital Poems, 'Upstairs Piano', he can write:

> And yet, and yet, men pale
> (Late under Passchendaele
> Or some such blot on earth)
> Feel once again the birth
> Of joy in them, and know
> That Beauty's not a show
> Of lovely things long past.

Music is a restorative for 'stricken men' who 'Take heart and glimpse the light'. What is the light, we may wonder? Gurney tells us. 'If they shall see the stars/More clearly after their wars,/That is a good wage.' I don't think it's forcing a point to suggest that Gurney envisages music as both symbolizing, and empowering men to imagine, a transformed because limitless universe. The stars are in some measure akin to Hazlitt's day-star of Liberty, or that 'new planet' at the end of Keats's 'On First Looking Into Chapman's Homer', not so much because Gurney consciously appeals to either of these Romantics as because his vision here, no matter how elusively expressed, is at once radical and optimistic. The 'good wage' coming to the men who see stars is, after all, definitely *not* to be thought of in utilitarian terms.

This brings me back to 'On Rest'. The men who see stars are conceivably the same men to whom 'On Rest' is dedicated,

ordinary soldiers who happen to belong in this instance to the 2/
5 Gloucester Regiment. Gurney's exuberant, comic, playful
poem is a celebration of ordinariness, of the dearness of
common things, and of course, of commonalty. Who else but
Gurney would manage to write so joyously about *breakfast*, for
goodness sake?

> The farmer's wife searching for eggs, 'midst all
> Dear farmhouse cries. A stroll: and then 'Breakfast's up.'
> Porridge and bacon! Tea out of a real cup
> (Borrowed).

The authentic Gurney note, that use of carry-over from line
ending to qualify ardour by knowingly comic let-down. (As in
the altogether greater 'The Silent One', 'and swore deep heart's
deep oaths/(Polite to God)').

There's no doubt that in discovering how to write this kind of
poem Gurney owed a considerable debt to Thomas. He certainly
couldn't have found elsewhere the means to handle a narrative
that starts from anecdote – often sparked by a happenstance
meeting, as in 'Lob' and 'As the Team's Head-Brass' – or in
which a stray occasion, a name, a glimpse of an object, a sound, a
sight, acts as trigger for thought processes that gradually
unwind to unforeknown conclusions. These conclusions can
be seen to build out of the apparently arbitrary details with
which the poems are crammed. They are included not merely
for their own sweet sake but because they *cohere*. Not that such
coherence is easily declared. More often than not, indeed, it is
elusive, like a hidden history.

Gurney touches on this in a letter to Marion Scott dated 18
May 1917, when he imagines himself back in his native county.
'And the first walk I shall take shall be Dymock, Newent, Ross
and into Wales, to end at Chepstow after meeting names met in
Malory; names known it would seem a thousand years ago in
some forgotten life stronger in charm than their realities of
houses and trees' (*Letters*, 261–2). He will make poems out of
such walks, as Thomas so magnificently did. But in France it's
the *present* which has to cohere, and, as 'On Rest' shows, this
means the little world of exhausted soldiers, men of the Glosters,
who nevertheless make 'our Commonwealth', where 'All's equal
now'. Here, 'Ragtimes and any kind of nonsense' exist alongside

the chaff and smile of officers, the estaminets' open doors, the higgledy-pigglediness of a prolonged moment of carnival where men may enjoy 'Dinner, perhaps a snooze, perhaps a stroll'. Coherence here is achieved not by order but by, well, not disorder, exactly, but by mutuality. For a commonwealth is composed of 'a group of persons united by some common interest'.

Towards the end of 'On Rest', Gurney evokes this common interest as the men's fierce desire: 'again to see the ricks, the farms/Blue roads, still trees of home'. From this we once more return to the present, to where 'the last/Candles are lit in bivvy and barn and cart,/Where comrades talking lie...' Except that it *isn't* the present. Because, as I've already noted, Gurney wrote the poem in the autumn of 1918, when he was back in England. This is important. I don't at all mean to suggest that retro-spectively Gurney invests the actual moment with a radical implication it didn't at the time possess. But there's no doubt that what he celebrates in writing about the commonwealth of comrades is precisely its radical nature. And that it was merely a moment, when men were 'On Rest', doesn't mean it can't be made into a more enduring vision. 'On Rest' is an intensely political poem. It opens up and celebrates far-reaching Demo-cratic Vistas.

The allusion to Whitman's famous work is intended. For if 'On Rest' owes much to Thomas – a debt also very evident in 'The Lock-Keeper', which is indeed dedicated to Thomas's memory – the poem also owes much to Whitman. And this is not merely in its readiness to sound a 'barbaric yawp' (though who but a lover of Whitman would speak of a 'snooze' or rejoice in 'outcries, catcalls, queries, doubtful wit'); there is also, empha-tically, Gurney's praise for Whitman, the 'lover of common men'. Gurney isn't included in Gregory Woods's splendid *History of Gay Literature*, but he might well have been. At all events, I do not see how you can read 'To His Love', and other poems besides, without recognizing their homo-erotic charge. 'To His Love' seems to have been written very early in 1918. On the face of it, the poem can be taken for one of those many laments for a young, beautiful male whose early death is at once tragic and proper. (Old, he'd have lost his looks.) The Emperor Hadrian's adored youth, Antinous, is the conventional archetype.

War has always provided an opportunity for such laments and, with *A Shropshire Lad* already in print and becoming increasingly popular, poets of the Great War had examples ready to hand. I don't know whether Gurney had anyone specifically in mind when he wrote 'To His Love'. He subtitled a draft of the poem 'On a Dead Soldier', but that doesn't tell us anything. It's notable, however, that the poem *isn't* dedicated to anyone in particular, whereas no fewer than thirty of the fifty-nine poems in *Severn & Somme* – thirty-one if we count the introductory verses to Marion Scott, – do have dedicatees. One way to read the poem, therefore, is as an attempt to forgo his own sexuality. The last stanza runs:

> Cover him, cover him soon!
> And with thick-set
> Masses of memoried flowers
> Hide that red wet
> Thing I must somehow forget.

Why must he forget? Can the admittedly short-lived relationship with nurse Annie Drummond, which preceded the writing of the poem, be adduced as further evidence of Gurney's attempted denial of his sexuality? But this is mere speculation, and in lacking a good up-to-date biography we lack so much knowledge about Gurney's life that there's not much point in pursuing the matter further.

What can be said is that 'To His Love' manages to renew the kind of pastoral elegy that finds expression in, for example, the dirge in *Cymbeline* ('Fear no more the heat o' the sun'), by adapting it to present circumstances.

> You would not know him now...
> But still he died
> Nobly, so cover him over
> With violets of pride
> Purple from Severn side.

That might serve as the final stanza, in which nature, too, bleeds. 'Purple from Severn side' implies that the flowers are bloodied by contact with the wounded side of a sacrificial body. But then comes the invocation to 'Cover him, cover him soon'. 'To His Love' is song-like; it generalizes or anyway avoids the particularity of more personal lyric poetry. As such, it becomes a fit elegy for any soldier killed away from home – which in this case is the Cotswolds. Indeed, the dead man doesn't ever need to be a soldier. He could be anyone dead before his time, as could the dead youth in Owen's marvellous little elegy 'Futility'. Gurney's decision to remove the subtitle 'On a dead soldier' suggests that he, too, might be more interested in the poem as a type of elegy rather than prompted by a particular person. And though that brutal word 'thing', which meets you as you come round the penultimate line-ending, is bound to jolt, it doesn't inevitably require to be thought of as occasioned by war. What matters is the placing of the word. Gurney may have taken it from Shakespeare ('this thing of darkness I acknowledge mine') or Hopkins (though that depends on the exact dating of the poem and when he got hold of the copy of Hopkins's poems lent him by Haines); but nobody taught him how to *use* the word with such extraordinary fervour. The dearness of this common thing is inseparable from a heart-piercing recognition that 'thing' is precisely what a man has become.

Moreover, the poem is song-like in other ways. A subtle weave of assonances is threaded right through, requiring the ear to detect a stress pattern that owes far more to the varying pulse of song than to regular repeated metric stress; this is enhanced by the device of unrhymed disyllabic end-words at the middle line of each stanza which enact a kind of musical pause. 'Impatient' and in a 'rush' Gurney might sometimes know himself to be, but, as he also knew, he could on occasion compose songs 'as tender as any of all that noble host' of great Elizabethan songs. 'To His Love' is one such song.

* * *

For all its elusiveness, 'To His Love' may be said to testify to what Wilfred Owen famously called 'the pity of war'. But *War's Embers* is by no means confined to elegy or poems of loss and regret. There are also, and I'd say more importantly because unique to Gurney, those poems which testify to comradeship and what comes of that: a desire to make a new world. Gurney's second collection is truly radical, not merely because of what it says but because of its break with those elements of Georgianism by which *Severn & Somme* had been largely constrained. To put it

31

rather differently, *War's Embers* represents a crucial break-through for English poetry. As he frees himself from the conventionalities on which many of the poems in his first collection depend, so Gurney finds a way of pursuing the urgent impellings of imaginative thought. He had earlier spoken ruefully and apologetically to Marion Scott about his lack of patience. But impatience can be a virtue. Certainly I can see nothing wrong with being 'unable or unwilling to endure or put up with something', which is how the *OED* defines the word, when that something is itself intolerable, as the continuation of war in order to serve the self-interest of politicians and armaments racketeers undoubtedly proved to be.

This leads to a further point. There is still a widely accepted orthodoxy of literary history according to which the new, modernist poetry of the 1920s was largely produced by poets who, for whatever reason, had not been to war. According to this orthodoxy, the great poem of the period, *The Waste Land*, is a diagnostic account of a broken world such as could be produced by no soldier-poet, because soldier-poets were either dead (Owen, Rosenberg, Edward Thomas) or so hurt by their experiences that they turned away from the post-war world, said *Goodbye to All That* (Robert Graves), or retreated into faded pastoralism (Blunden, Sassoon), or into myth-making as a way of incorporating the events of 1914–18 into a long narrative of human history under divine control (David Jones). No matter how adequate or otherwise this orthodoxy is to the poets mentioned, it very plainly won't help when we try to think about Gurney. For this reason, no doubt, few who write about the period have much, if anything, to say about a poet who, unlike virtually all the other war-poets, fought as a line soldier, and whose experiences of the war he survived perhaps awoke and certainly confirmed a radicalism which required him to make poetry very different from most of what he saw around him. To put the matter this way is, I hope, to indicate that Gurney ought to be seen as *at least* as valid a presence in post-war poetry as Eliot.

2

1919–1922

As soon as the Armistice came into operation, on 11 November 1918, Gurney finished work at the munitions factory where he had been employed. During his time there he had made several attempts to go to sea, and friends became worried by what they recognized as increasingly erratic behaviour. A deep restlessness begins increasingly now to show itself, as a brief summary of the outward events of the next three years makes plain.

In January 1919, after spending Christmas in Cornwall, he returns to the Royal College of Music and takes digs in West Kensington. By late February, he is back in Gloucester, at the family home, correcting proofs of *War's Embers*. Towards the end of April he begins work as an unskilled labourer at Dryhill Farm, Shurdington (near Stroud), although this doesn't last long, because by the middle of May he is back in London, now living at St John's Wood. Then, in September, he takes a post as organist at Christ Church, High Wycombe. This also proves to be short-lived. But during the autumn of 1919, and despite suffering from 'nerves and an inability to think or write at all clearly', he makes some attempt to break into London literary circles. He also pays a visit to John Masefield, then living at Boar's Hill, Oxford. Also on Boar's Hill at that time were Robert Bridges and Robert Graves, although there's no evidence that Gurney met either poet.

The following year, drawn back to Dryhill, he tries to set up a cottage at Cold Slad. Not surprisingly that doesn't work out and he returns to to lodgings in London's Earls Court. By April 1921 he is back in Gloucester, from where, in June, he moves to

Stokenchurch, near High Wycombe. He now formally leaves the Royal College of Music and yet again returns to Gloucester, where, living at his aunt's house, he once more takes up farm work. At the tail end of the year he accepts a post as pianist in a cinema at Bude, but lasts a mere week.

Early January 1922 finds him living in Waltham Green, London. He then moves to Plumstead, south of the river, and again finds work playing the piano in a cinema. This time he lasts two weeks; after which, it's back to his aunt's house, and more farm work. All this time he has been writing poetry and, for the most part, failing to get it published. In May 1922 he submits a collection of eighty poems to Sidgwick & Jackson, who return it with the suggestion that he prune and revise. He also gains and loses a succession of farm jobs.

On 3 July, a few days after Sidgwick & Jackson reject his re-submitted collection of poems, he begins work in the Gloucester Tax Office, a job that lasts for twelve weeks. In September, he moves in unannounced with his brother and sister-in-law in Gloucester. His behaviour now becomes increasingly wild, erratic, and culminates in attempts at suicide. On 28 September he is certified insane and admitted to Barnwood House, a private asylum near Gloucester. A month later he escapes, is recaptured, escapes again – it is now November – and finally, on 21 December, is transferred to the City of London Mental Hospital at Dartford. He will remain there until his death on 26 December 1937.

Even so bald a summary will indicate how restlessly perturbed a spirit Gurney's was. Yet we should not be misled into thinking that his post-war inability to settle either to occupation or place was at all unusual. As Arnold Rattenbury remarks in his seminal essay 'How the Sanity of Poets Can Be Edited Away', 'Academic societies are always special after a war. Uniquely experienced, horribly experienced, people return to institutions which innocents from school and cathedral are entering for the first time. ... Gurney managed only one year back at the Royal College of Music, his fellow ex-soldier-poet [Edgell] Rickword only one year at Oxford.'[1] No, it isn't the unsettledness that needs to be especially remarked. But the endless shuttling between country and city, and between exercising his professional skill as a pianist and choosing to work as a farm labourer, that *is* unusual, that *does* tell us about Gurney's desperate uncertainties, or perhaps his aching desire for an identity which would reconcile those seemingly irreconcilable elements: urban, pastoral, intellectual, labourer, man apart, comrade and fellow.

And, as I say, all the time he was writing poetry. (He was also writing music, but here I lack both space and competence to follow him.) Poems went off to leading periodicals and usually came back. *Severn & Somme* was reprinted in early 1919, but the greatly superior *War's Embers*, published in May of that year, was coolly received and sold poorly. No further collection appeared during his lifetime. Yet in 1924 he listed the titles of no fewer than seven books which he claimed to have written or which were on the stocks: *Rewards of Wonder; Dayspaces and Takings; Ridge Clay, Limestone; La Flandre, and By-Norton; Roman Gone East; London Seen Clear; Fatigues and Magnificences*. In the Introduction to their edition of *Best Poems and the Book of Five Makings*, Kelsey Thornton and George Walter remark that 'We know only the first of these. The others were perhaps sent out, but to no effect.'[2]

It was once thought that *Rewards of Wonder* must have been the collection which, in different versions, Gurney submitted to Sidgwick & Jackson in 1922. Thornton and Walter's labours have shown that this isn't the case. The poems Gurney's publishers saw are, in fact, those that make up what his editors call *80 Poems or So*. They have reconstituted this collection, although in grouping the poems thematically they have, as Rattenbury complains, produced a book as unlikely as it is unlovely. 'This is not the way Gurney assembled himself, either in the two volumes he published or in other draft collections.'[3]

Rattenbury is right. The pell-mell nature of Gurney's mind, his desire to make connections between country and city (say) and music and poetry, is muffled if we separate out poems about Gloucestershire from London poems. This isn't to deny that on occasion Gurney could try on a mode he didn't much care about, in order to win the approval of literary editors. John Clare had done much the same thing a hundred years earlier, and his reward was to have had some decidedly routine poems published in the kinds of Annuals and Keepsakes which were fashionable in the 1820s and 1830s. And why not? They put money in a pocket that was usually empty. I doubt that Gurney did it for the money, but a poem such as 'Fine Rain', published in the *Nation* in 1921, is about as conventional as post-war Gurney ever gets. It's not much more than the kind of 'London Sketch' you can find in many a Georgian anthology. 'There's mirth in London streets,/Where the rain fleets/To silver every fur', is how the poem starts. But this isn't the way Gurney typically writes of London streets, where, after all, ex-soldiers are walking 'sore in borrowed tatterns/Or begged' ('Strange Hells'), and where 'Gaol waits' for the boys of 'that evil smelling/Township' ('North Woolwich'). And to say this brings me to the heart of the matter.

Matthew Arnold famously thought a poet should try to banish from his mind 'all feelings of contradiction, and irritation, and impatience'. These are the very feelings out of which some of the greatest writers forge their art. Gurney is, I think, among them, but in making this claim I need to add that irritation and impatience don't at all make for incoherence, though neither do they make for the Arnoldian desideratum of seeing life steadily and whole. Gurney's preoccupations – with the Cotswolds, London, Music, Poetry, the War, Labour – seize hold of him differently at different times. There are shifts of emphasis, of perspective. Moreover, he only gradually comes to commit himself as overwhelmingly to poetry as to music. Thinking of this, I'm reminded of the Irish poet Patrick Kavanagh saying: 'you begin by making verses and later discover it's become your life'. That this is true for Gurney will explain why, in the years following 1919, his poetry becomes increasingly the medium for attesting to all he cares most deeply about. It also explains why, without in any sense being disloyal to such early literary models as Gibson and F. W. Harvey, he knows he can profit far more from studying Hopkins and Edward Thomas. Whatever doubts and uncertainties plagued him, he knew, deep in the core of his being, that he was a true poet. At the head of the collection *Best Poems*, which he was assembling in 1924–5, he identified himself as *First War Poet*. Then, characteristically, he added in brackets '(He does truly believe)'. By 'first' he doesn't mean poet of the First World War, a label which only became attached to 1914–18 after 1945. He means quite simply that he's the first true poet of that war. And while he guards against a charge of over-reading by pinioning his claim within brackets – not to tempt providence – it's nevertheless seriously intended. Hence, his putting himself to school to study poets he knows are of true importance.

Gurney's admiration for Thomas is well documented in the *Letters*. His interest in Hopkins is a different matter. References crop up infrequently, and at first aren't at all favourable. But then, it took Gurney some time to recognize Thomas's especial worth. (Still, that recognition was lightning fast compared with those for whom Thomas could – *can still* – be lumped in with the Georgians.) Gradually, however, Hopkins clearly came to mean a great deal to him. In an article which first appeared in the *Gloucester Journal* in 1935, and which was reprinted in no. 1 of the *Ivor Gurney Society Journal* (1995), Gurney's friend John Haines recalls that in the immediate post-war period he lent Gurney books 'which put him in touch with the work of Edward Thomas and Gerard Manley Hopkins, the two modern poets he most admired and those who contributed most to his literary technique'.

I've already touched on those aspects of Gurney's verse-making that owe much to Thomas's example. As to Hopkins, it's evident that the greater suppleness – informality, I want to say – of Gurney's rhythms in his post-war writing is prompted by his reading of Hopkins, as is some of his phrasing. A letter of March/April 1919 to Marion Scott contains a poem 'My County' – it hasn't been collected – in which Gurney writes of seeking out 'quiet places/Hidden by hedgerow, havens each a story'. Here the emphatic alliteration and caesura break followed by heavy stress – *hav*ens – are plainly devices taken from Hopkins (*Letters*, 479). Or consider 'April 20, 1919' (in *80 Poems or So*), which rejoices in the springtime world, in an intense registering of its 'realty' through sight and sound, through 'Beauty which swells the bud' and 'fills/The blackbird so with untoucht wonder of love,/He sings in the vale to awaken the echoing hills'. A fussy editor could point to echoes of the Psalms, of Blake, and of Keats. But that little word 'so' is precisely the intensifier that Hopkins made memorably his own in 'Spring', where he writes of how 'thrush/Through the echoing timber does so rinse and wring/The ear'.

There are other such debts. As Thornton and Walter point

out, the word 'realty', which Gurney uses on two occasions (in 'Fragment' and 'On a Town', both in *80 Poems or So*), is to be found in Hopkins's 'Duns Scotus Oxford', where the philosopher whom Hopkins tendentiously praised for his delight in the natural world, its 'thisness', is called 'Of realty the rarest-veined unraveller'. But where Hopkins's heart in hiding 'stirred for a bird', in 'Fragment', Gurney, grappling with his own dark depression, finds 'Realty have never margin for desire,/And matter's the true business of the soul'. 'Realty' for him, then, in this particular poem, exerts an inescapable pressure of 'griefs of roughest kind'. Gurney does not have Hopkins's means of clambering from what, in one of the 'terrible' sonnets, the poet-priest called the 'cliffs of fall/Frightful, sheer, no-man-fathomed'. But there seems no reason to doubt that he recognized in Hopkins a mental distress in many ways similar to his own and one he courageously explored in a number of harrowing poems.

I don't, however, want to point the present discussion in that direction, not because I doubt the intensity of Gurney's mental anguish, but because he himself thought the proper business of poets was to engage with the peopled world we wake up to every day. In their different modes, Thomas and Hopkins were poets whose awareness of emotional and mental instability and of apartness from others strengthened their commitment to those others. Gurney couldn't have known of Hopkins's famous 'Red' letter to Robert Bridges – 'Horrible to say, in a manner I am a communist', but the poet who began 'The Lock-Keeper' by saying 'Men delight to praise men' would have felt kinship with the celebrant of Felix Randall, of Harry Ploughman and, given the homoeroticism so evident in Hopkins's work even though commentators so long denied it, with the poet who ecstatically celebrates 'The Bugler's First Communion'.

In several ways, then, Hopkins was a help. But there's no need to overstate the matter. For there are also sharp differences. Though Gurney delights in imagining young men of 'smoothly running muscle' who 'would face without a stitch// Heaven's nakedness', those 'boys' – his word – come from North Woolwich. Hopkins couldn't write about the city without lapsing into cliché. In a poem of 1887, 'Tom's Garland: upon the Unemployed', he reduces the out-of-work to 'Manwolf' whose 'packs infest the age'. Thirty years later, Gurney makes use of the word 'throng' and its variants to suggest not so much a pack of wolves as a fair field full of folk. No infestation here.

In a letter to Harvey, written in February 1918, when his friend was still a prisoner of war, Gurney asks him: 'Do you remember how, in Spring evenings, the gold of late sunlight used to be heavy on the floor of the orchard...And great sunsets? And autumn afterglows, most tender, most "thronged"? (You know what I mean.)' (*Letters*, 400) The word turns up in two poems from *80 Poems or So*: 'Before Resurrection' and 'Western Sky-Look'. The former is a Shelleyan-like invocation to a new spirit invading the world:

> The wind of March is out,
>   Sense of daffodils
> Through the quick blood thrills,
>   Glories, hurries about.
>
> The wind is royal yet,
>   Far royaller
> The memory of her
>   That Winter's cruelty set
> In frost-chains, she so eager,
>   And the violet.
>
> The blue and golden must
>   Time endure somehow
> Till March blow dust
>   In clouds, and the glow
>
> Of the sun draw shadows
>   Black-hard, strong;
> And over meadows
>   Skylarks throng.

At one level this exquisite lyric is undoubtedly about the cyclic return of life in a pastoral landscape. But the poem must have come at a time when Gurney was again planning to throw himself into farm work. (Marion Scott identifies it as having been written in 'Gloucestershire Feb or March 1919'.) On 22 April, he writes to Scott to tell her that he's taken up a post at Dryhill Farm and is 'set to learn farm business, to become sane and glad for life...'. While there, presumably, he wrote 'Above Dryhill', in which he records that

> the high wild hedges saw I tamed
> And cunning woven when the green buds flamed
> With deft inweaving like a player's showing
> Of Bach's fourstranded thought,
> Fixed pattern wrought
> So easy and as cunning to move wonder.

Gurney returns to this comparison of hedger and musician/composer in a poem of late 1922, which opens, 'To me the A Major Concerto has been dearer/Than ever before, because I saw one weave/Wonderful patterns of bright green'; it ends with the claim that 'never have I known singer piano-player/So quick and sure in movement as this hedge-layer/This gap-mender, of quiet courage unhastening' ('Hedger', Kavanagh, 161).

To speak like this is to avow the propriety of 'life and toil, with the actual troublous life of every day, with toil of the hands and brain together...' This is Edward Thomas extolling William Morris, and I have argued in an essay in *The Ivor Gurney Society Journal* in 1998 that Gurney is to be identified with Thomas's socialist reverence for Morris. ('Except William Morris, there is no other man I would sometimes like to have been.') Hence, such poems as 'The Hoe Scrapes Earth', 'Felling a Tree', 'Hedges', and 'The Mangel-bury'. The exultant tone of 'Before Resurrection' can, then, and I'd say *should* be, read as metaphor for a rebirth of what, in a poem called 'The Golden Age', Gurney will identify as a time of 'men working freely as nature might show...on a free soil'. That poem seems to have been written sometime late in 1922, but it voices a constant in Gurney's poetry: the desire for the kind of communities the great socialist R. H. Tawney repeatedly imagined as not merely adumbrated in Elizabethan England (his, as Gurney's, Golden Age) but achievable, out there, waiting to be brought into being, awaiting its Resurrection.

This ardent longing for a new world or, perhaps more accurately, a world made new recurs in 'Western Sky-Look', first published in the *Nation and Athenaeum* on 20 August 1921, but conceivably written at about the time Gurney was making one of his periodic attempts to find work at sea. It begins:

> When clouds shake out their sails
> Before delighted gales,
> I think the sailor-men at sea,
> Hearing the engine throbbing free
> Curse their today's fate that they must
> Defeat Magellan with black dust,
> Scrape deck-plates till the nerves are worn –;

Here, he goes on, is 'never work that's fit for man'. Why not? Because 'here and now pale Duty does/Domestic service on bright brass...' It's not that the sailors have now to do women's work which draws Gurney's anger; it's that their work is not pleasure, not challenge, but Duty, duty moreover to what's very plainly a dehumanizing process. And so, protesting instinctively against the strange hell of such wearisome labour,

> The sailor-men lift heart and eyes
> To the thronged skies:
> They cleave the air, leap winged to shake
> More sails, more sails out; watch the wake
> Of cirrus lengthen on the blue,
> And run clean sailor-work to do....
> Fall sheer... to waste and paraffin –
> Pistons gone tired of out-and-in,
> Black work as hard and dull as sin.

Looking west, where Shelley had searched for the world's new springtime, the sailors see 'thronged skies' – presumably those cirrus clouds which presage change, and which, by metaphoric extension, can be imagined as new life pouring in. Writing at more or less the same moment, Eliot saw such life as a threat, as 'hooded hordes' who emerge to infest (that word again) civilization. And for Yeats, they coalesce into the 'rough beast' of history. For Gurney, on the other hand, and for the sailors, 'thronged skies', whether or no we see them as the horsemen of the Apocalypse or as like Shelley's 'Angels of rain and lightning', signal new hope. A throng is no more a pack than, shall we say, a crowd is a mob. The sailors fall back to a world of black work, 'hard and dull as sin', but the vision remains. As Arnold Rattenbury acutely remarks, 'It is change Gurney is after, and spring means change to him, suddenness, urgency'.

Rattenbury goes on to suggest that the undated poem called 'Spring Dawn' in *80 Poems or So* ('Smudgy Dawn' in Kavanagh),

41

will be about the spring of 1920, 'during which socialism turned militant'. This seems entirely plausible, especially as the poem, which ends with the sun as 'fireswinger promised behind elm-pillars/Showed of a day worthy of such dawn to come after', does not merely produce this fierce sun as harbinger of change, but also finds room to note 'Birds a multitude: increasing as it made lighter'. Another throng. But, as Rattenbury also suggests, the companion piece to 'Spring Dawn' is very probably 'Coming Dusk', though the two are separated in *80 Poems or So* by an editorial decision which groups poems according to apparent theme. And in 'Coming Dusk', as at the end of 'Western Sky-Look', promise, or what Rattenbury calls 'joyous anticipation', is followed by doubt. Just as, we might note, the promise of spring, 1920, when the dockers refused to load onto ships armaments intended for the White Army in Poland, was followed by defeats of the following year, when, on 15 April, 'Black Friday', the promised Triple Alliance of Miners, Railwaymen and Transport Workers failed to materialize. As a result, the miners had to accept wage cuts forced on them by owners who'd just had the mines returned to their control after war-time nationalization. This doesn't mean that 'Coming Dusk' was written in April 1920, but does mean that when Gurney says 'In April has there come November's hour', and that 'Dumb Spring without a sign waits the day coming', he's acutely aware that making change happen isn't an easy matter.

Yet change was being made, at local, community level. And it was happening precisely in that part of England which Gurney knew best. That he could have been unaware of various Tolstoyan or otherwise utopian-minded communities, many of which had established themselves across the Cotswolds in the time he was growing up there, seems scarcely conceivable. It isn't only that his numerous poems about or mentioning craftskills must have come from *somewhere*, it's quite simply that people talked about these communities. They were common knowledge. So much so indeed that when, sometime in the 1920s, the Home Office decided to infiltrate the Whiteway Community, which was spread around an acreage of farmed land near Stroud, and although the husband-and-wife team who acted as agents were able to report back that 'Promiscuous fornication seems to be a prominent feature of the life of the place', the then Home Secretary, Joynson-Hicks, decided it would be safer to do nothing. 'The resulting agitation', he noted in a memo recently revealed, 'may lead to an even greater congregation of undesirables.' (In *The Independent*, Friday, 2 March 2000.) There's no doubt that Gurney is close in spirit to the ideals from which these various communities sprouted. Moreover, as Rattenbury has noted, the people Gurney met at the Royal College were by and large committed socialists.

> Vaughan Williams's colleague and friend Gustav Holst had joined William Morris's Hammersmith Socialist League in 1895... Vaughan Williams had been a socialist since his student days in Cambridge. Early on in relationship with Gurney he introduced him, presumably sensing a coincidence of interest, to Rutland Boughton, whose Glastonbury Festivals just before and after the First World War had been founded on communitarian (not to say, wife-sharing) principles and largely amateur forces (accompanied often by poultry.)

And Eric Hobsbawm has pointed to the widespread connection between socialism and the avant-garde in the years 1880–1914. As he remarks, 'the link was direct and conscious, especially in the British arts-and-crafts movement, whose great master William Morris became a sort of Marxist and made both a powerful theoretical as well as an outstanding practical contribution to the social transformation of the arts.'[4]

This transformation was happening more widely across England than has been often understood. Gurney undoubtedly encountered it in London, but, to repeat, he must also have met with it in those many expressions of what Mary Greensted calls the *Arts and Crafts Movement in the Cotswolds*, which she writes about in her monograph, published by Sutton, 1993. We might also note that Clive Aslet has a fascinating account of Detmar Blow's attempt to establish a soviet at his house – Hilles it was called – which Blow built in rural Gloucestershire.[5] And in *Back to the Land: The Pastoral Impulse in England, from 1880 to 1914*, Jan Marsh has much to say about those Agrarian communities which typically emphasized the values of 'comradeship, honesty, the abjuration of all forms of violence and coercion'.[6] Shades of the comradeship of those 'On Rest' where, 'Authority forgotten, all goes well/In this our Commonwealth'. Shades, too, of the Dymock Poets, those acquaintances of Gurney whose spirit was essentially comunitarian and, in its own way, utopian.

II

Lacking as we do an up-to-date biography, the progress of Gurney's thought can't, I think, be traced with any degree of exactness. Nor does it much matter. The Cotswold communities, friendships formed at the Royal College of Music, reading Whitman for the first time, a growing sense that the war was becoming 'the bosses' war' (that, certainly), anger over the plight of returned veterans, at the condition of the poor in London's East End and elsewhere: some of these happen in synchronicity, others overlap, still others gradually assume importance. That's how it always is. But the poet who in 1919 welcomed the throng of skylarks in 'Before Resurrection' is not quite the same poet who sees people 'Thronging the streets' of his native city, and who feels separate from and, in a not very laudable sense, superior to them. ('But none thought of old/Gloucester blood brought,/Loved so the City/As I the poet unthought.' How can he *know*?)

The intellectual's and artist's feeling of 'innate' superiority to others is easily enough come by in our society, so much so that it is naturalized into a conviction of absolute difference. Coleridge's belief that beautiful sights and sounds are to the peasant 'pictures to the blind and music to the deaf' lives on. But Gurney's experience of trench warfare, allied to other experiences and discoveries mentioned above, gradually brought him to realize its malign absurdity. Hence, his praise of the Hedger, already alluded to, whose

> quick moving
> Was never broken by any danger, his loving
> Use of the bill or scythe was most deft, and clear –
> Had my piano-playing or counterpoint
> Been so without fear
> Then indeed fame had been mine of most bright outshining;
> But never have I known singer or piano-player
> So quick and sure in movement as this hedge-layer
> This gap-mender, of quiet courage unhastening.

You could, of course, argue that Gurney's intermittent poems in praise of rural labour at best honour country craft, at worst endorse a misty-eyed myth of the rural as the natural. And it is true there is something touchingly comic about this gawky and

44

physically uncoordinated man trying to work alongside agrarian craftsmen. (Though he was a good footballer and a crack shot.) But there's nothing the least bit comic about his refusal to condescend to them. And besides, his concern is not merely with agricultural labourers but with those who work – labour – in the city. He speaks for all, and no doubt takes the idea from them, from what he's experienced working with them, when he praises 'The mind that's always good when let go its way/(I think) so there's work enough in a happy day'. That entirely characteristic use of enjambement to set up a moment of doubt, contained as it is by brackets, directs us to the fact that 'A wish', from which the lines come, was written in October 1922, by which time Gurney was locked up. But we must then note that there's no dwelling on self-pity here. The belief in the desirability of work enough is what counts. *This* is what makes for a happy day.

Gurney is however writing out of post-war England, when for many men and women the possibility of such happiness appears infinitely remote. It certainly seemed so to 'the children of West Ham', for whom Gurney breathes his Wish, a matter to which I shall return. Here, I want to note how often, from 1919 onward, he writes about London and that, if we leave aside those conventional, Georgian 'sketches' of London scenes, his engagement with the city is at one with his writing about rural circumstances. Hence, for example, 'Town-Thoughts from Severn', to be found in *80 Poems or So*, where Gurney turns London into a city pastoral, 'March clouds up-piled like sighted thunder,/Onslow Square, delicate with cherry snow'. The poem ends with the insistent claim that

> Costers and coal-heavers
> Have courage, Will-to-Life as high as any
> Dwellers by hills, valleys, or tiny rivers,
> Be it Fretherne, Bredon Hill or Abergavenny!

Moreover, as Rattenbury points out, one poem in particular, 'The Road' (not in Kavanagh but in *80 Poems or So*), powerfully reveals, indeed is *about*, Gurney's refusal to wedge apart the urban and rural radical traditions. It starts 'Out beyond Aldgate is a road,/A broad, clean noble thing it runs,/For the sun's/And wind's and man's delight', and soon this road becomes a

45

thoroughfare thronged – the word is appropriate – by all sorts
and conditions of men and women. If English Utopianism
traditionally envisages a field full of folk, its modern counterpart
needs to celebrate a *road* full of folk: of 'Jewesses/And Poles and
Russ and these/Pale-faced sons', all of whom endure 'A hard
life, hardly earned; Routine that galls...' But the throng is
intensely alive. Come the weekend and there's

> Thunder
> Of trams and buses crammed,
> Or Saturday-night dammed-
> Up, seething, dodging,
> Grumbling, laughing, over-busy
> Crowd in Mile End crammed;
> Or in one hour of joys
> When football plays
> Marvellous music on these jigging heart-strings,
> And one lucky kick brings
> Battle-winning in a Niagara of noise...

This wondrous helter-skelter, with its this-way-that-way account
of London crowds – it even includes what must be about the first
acknowledgement in poetry of football's importance for city folk
– makes clear that, *pace* the *Waste Land*, death *cannot* have undone
so many. Nonetheless, Gurney registers what's lacking from
lives galled by routine. The poems ends – I have to quote at
length:

> Anyhow folk live there
> And daily strive there,
> And earn their bread there,
> Make friends, see red there
> As high on the clean hills
> Where soft sea-rapture fills
> The gladdening lungs.
> And young souls are fleshed there
> And tyrant immeshed there
> As in Athens or Ukraine.
> And the heart hurts the brain
> Or the spirit is lashed there,
> And thought is as vain,
> Hope constant, and smashed there,
> As away a day's journey by train.

The area of the East End Gurney has in mind, around the Commercial Road and leading to North Woolwich, is richly cosmopolitan, a place of 'anyhow folk'. (I take it that by calling them 'folk', Gurney is not being down-home or 'folksy', and thus running the risk of condescension; he uses the word to indicate that they *do* come from various places – all those places where 'the folk' are to be found.) 'The Road' both celebrates them and acknowledges that their dreams of immeshing tyrants are repeatedly smashed. Yet a new world is reachable: as near, or far, as a day's journey by train.

'The Road' was published in *The Spectator* in March 1923, but must have been written earlier. Thornton and Walter don't offer a possible date, but I'm pretty certain that the poem will have been written sometime in 1920. Until the fall of Germany, the Ukraine had been under a puppet German ruler, Hetman. It was then taken over by Denikin; Pilsudski captured Kiev for the Poles in May 1920, and finally, in the summer of that year, the Red Army took control of the region. This is the moment when the London dockers refuse to load arms intended for the 'White Army' in Poland. The folk whom Gurney writes about included dockers. But *all* of them 'see red'. And of course the CPGB (Communist Party of Great Britain) was formed in 1920. Could anyone reading the poem in 1923 have been unaware of the train journey that had brought Lenin to revolutionary power?

At the beginning of a poem written after his incarceration, 'First Time In', Gurney muses that 'After the dread tales and red yarns of the Line/Anything might have come to us'. I take it he means that line soldiers he was among talked revolution; and anyone wanting to think he's here guilty of imputing to war years what belongs to a later moment has only to remember 'To the Prussians of England' in order to realize that dissident, angry, socialist, 'red', voices were very plainly making themselves heard in the trenches. One of them was Gurney's. His anger, then, at what happened to those who'd fought and returned home to penury, neglect, humiliation, is not merely articulate in such poems as 'Strange Hells', with its grieving rage on behalf of those on 'State-doles, or showing shop-patterns/Or walking town to town sore in borrowed tatterns/Or begged' (again the enjambement driving home the terrible indignity so many returned soldiers had to endure), it conditions his deepest thinking. As he says there, 'Some civic routine one never learns./The heart burns – but has to keep out of face how heart burns.' You can read this as a shamefaced admission of the need to stay polite in order to get a job. You can also read it as implying the need for silence and cunning, those tactics which Lenin recommended to those engaged in building the revolution.

The other tactic Lenin recommended was exile. I hope it isn't twisting words unduly if I suggest that much of Gurney's poetry seems to me to engage with and explore a condition close to exile and which would later become known as alienation. The root meaning of alien is 'a person owing allegiance to another country than the one in which he lives', while an exile is 'a person banished or living away from his home or country'. This has a considerable bearing on 'North Woolwich'.

The poem, to be found in *80 Poems or So*, was presumably written some time between 1921 and 1922, at all events if we accept Thornton and Walter's suggestion that the manuscript notebook in which it appears, and which gives on its cover the address '1 Westfield Terrace, Longford, Gloucester', can be dated to that period. I mention this because it then becomes evident that despite the editors' decision to place 'North Woolwich' immediately after 'The Road', they aren't really companion pieces. A mere glance at the poems themselves will confirm that this is so. For where in 'The Road' revolutionary energy seems only a day's train-ride away, the tone of 'North Woolwich' is altogether more sombre, even resigned.

> Can Aphrodite bless so evil dwelling.
>
> Or Mercury have heed to Canning Town?
> Nay, rather, for that ugly, evil smelling
> Township, One Christ from Heaven should come down,
>
> Pitiful and comradely with tender signs,
> And hot the tea, and shield a chap from fines,
> A foreman carpenter not yet full grown.

The allusions to Aphrodite and Mercury (it should really be Hermes) are there because the poem begins with 'Hellene memories barbed of the bright/Morning of new Time among tall derricks'. From the golden dawn of civilization to this! 'For Sappho's easy happy mirth the cackle/Brittle that's not of help to odes or lyrics.' Thornton and Walter gloss this as follows: 'He encounters noise that is not so conducive to poetry as that round Sappho, the Greek lyric poetess of the seventh century BC'. But lyric and ode don't exhaust the possibilities of poetry. There is also epic, for example, and that this must have been in Gurney's mind is made very plain in the following lines, where he notes

> Houses like long Iliadian lines stretch on
> And railing shadows bar a recognisable
> Of-no-man-questioned earth, whose chemistry

> To Marathon or Sparta kin must be.
> The vault of air as stable
> As on Olympus ringed with careless vines
> Or where Ithaca seaward green inclines.

Here, the distinction between ancient Greece and modern London matters far less than the connections. Marathon and Sparta were places of epic struggle between opposing forces.

Yet Gurney rather turns away from the possibility of struggle. Instead, he mourns the waste of speed and cunning, of those qualities associated especially with Achilles and Odysseus, in 'boys' who cannot show 'that smoothly running muscle./Gaol waits for them would face without a stitch//Heaven's naked- ness; those feet are black as pitch/Should gleam on gold sands white or in Stadium lines.' Without a hint of Hopkins's censoriousness, though with something of his homoeroticism, Gurney imagines the male youths of early twentieth-century Canning Town as not unlike the packs of manwolf who infest the end of 'Tom's Garland: Upon the Unemployed'. Unlike the folk who throng the road, however, or his soldier-comrades, they can be saved, not by seeing red, nor by their own efforts, but by Christ, who 'should come down' ('must' in Kavanagh's text), to shield a chap from fines.

This may owe something to the Christian socialism which Gurney would almost certainly have encountered in his early days at the Royal College of Music – it was strong in London in the opening years of the twentieth century; and the 'pitiful and comradely' Christ has more than a suggestion of Whitman about him. There may also be a glance at George Lansbury's decision, taken in September 1921 with twenty-nine other councillors, to face prison rather than levy the London County Council's unrealistically high rates on the impoverished folk of Poplar. Lansbury was a Christian pacifist as well as a socialist. But however we try to read the closing lines of 'North Woolwich', I think we have to say that the foreman carpenter, 'not yet full grown', is not merely an unlikely intercessor, as Gurney himself admits (hence the desperate 'should' or, if you prefer, 'must'), but that this represents a moment of something like defeatism.

If so, it isn't to be wondered at. Assuming the poem to have been written in late 1921 or early 1922, as seems most likely, and also assuming that it was written while Gurney was in Gloucester, we have to note that he had by then given up the Royal College, that he was finding it increasingly difficult to get his poems published, that he couldn't hold down a regular job, and that in all respects, therefore, his own position seemed decidedly precarious. Still more important, I suspect, is the fact that the bright hopes of 1920 had in the following months given way to repeated failures of organized labour. As I have earlier noted, and now need to spell out, in the spring of 1921 came the opportunity for what to all intents and purposes would have been a general strike. On 31 March the miners were locked out by mine owners, to whom the mines had been handed back by the government following war-time nationalization, and who immediately insisted on heavy cuts in wages. The Railwaymen and Transport Workers agreed to begin a sympathetic strike on Saturday, 16 April. Let Henry Pelling explain what happened next.

> On Friday 15th April, the day before his union was due to join the strike, J. H. Thomas of the Railwaymen demanded that the Miners should resume negotiation; and on their refusal, he and Robert Williams of the Transport Workers cancelled the sympathetic strike. The Miners stayed out; but they felt they had been 'betrayed' by their allies, and 15 April 1921 was thereafter known as 'Black Friday.' At the end of June the Miners were forced to give way, accepting heavy cuts in their wages.[7]

Although there were mines near Gurney in the Forest of Dean and the South Wales he regularly invokes in his poetry, the events of spring 1921 may at first glance seem remote from 'North Woolwich'. But it's worth recalling that during his time in the trenches Gurney had come into friendly contact with Welsh soldiers, a matter he celebrates in two poems which bear the same title, 'First Time In'. Kavanagh puts both poems in his selection from *Rewards of Wonder (Collected 1919–1920)*, but, in his Everyman selection, Walter places the first of them among poems which, while perhaps intended for *Rewards of Wonder*, may well be of later date. This deserves further comment.

The incident from which both poems start can be found in a letter Gurney addressed to Marion Scott, dated 7 June 1916.

> But O what luck! Here I am in a signal dugout with some of the nicest, and most handsome young men I ever met. And would you believe it? my luck I mean; they talk their native language and sing their own folksongs with sweet natural voices. I did not sleep at all for the first day in the dugout there was too much to be said, asked, and experienced; and the pleasure in watching their quick expressions for oblivion. It was one of the notable evenings of my life...
>
> ...these few days in the signal dugout with my Cymric friends are of the happiest for years. Out of the company to an extent we breathe the air of freedom almost forgotten...
>
> They sang David of the White Rock, and the Slumber Song...And O their voices! I thank God for the experience. (*Letters*, 86-87)

The process by which the events recorded in this letter were transmuted into poetry has been carefully traced by Rennie Parker in an important article in the *Ivor Gurney Society Journal* (vol. 5, 1999). We can therefore be sure that the experience for which Gurney thanked God took firm hold on his imagination. Soon afterwards he began to try to turn it into poetry, but it took many drafts and several more years before he was at all satisfied with his efforts. At first, he tries merely to report the encounter with the Welsh 'boys' as accurately as he can. Then he begins to develop the idea of comradeship. Finally, he comes to acknowledge or at least allow for the possible closing down of those hopes for the ideal of a good society which the vision of comradeship had opened up.

It is therefore significant that Walter provisionally dates the poem he prints as belonging to August 1923. Given this, it might be thought more appropriate for me to discuss the poem in the next chapter. But this would be to dislocate it from the context to which it clearly belongs: of Gurney's continually evolving recollections of war and of the sense to be made of them. The poem is both of the war in its vivid celebration of his encounter with the Welsh soldiers, and post-war in its feeling for the possible evanescence of that vision of comradeship opened up to him by the meeting and, very tellingly, because of voices in harmony.

'After the dread tales and red yarns of the line/Anything might have come to us', the poem begins. Do dread tales and red yarns oppose each other? Almost certainly. On the one hand, stories of war's horror, on the other, of (who knows?) mutiny, resistance, of doing in the Prussians of England. There is nothing about these yarns in Gurney's letter to Marion Scott. This doesn't necessarily mean that they weren't spoken – he had the official censor to consider in whatever he told her of trench talk – but the chances are that in 1916 the phrase 'red yarns' wouldn't have come readily to mind. Looking back on the encounter, though, Gurney might well have realized that what he and his mates were talking about could be covered by the phrase. Moreover, from those yarns Gurney and company move out of Line to 'a Welsh colony/Hiding in sandbag ditches',

> and there but boys gave kind welcome
> So that we looked out as though from the edge of home,
> Sang us Welsh things, and changed all former notions
> To human hopeful things...
> Candles they gave us – precious and shared over-rations –
> Ulysses found little more in his wanderings without doubt.
> 'David of the white rock', the 'Slumber Song' so soft, and that
> Beautiful tune to which roguish words by Welsh pit boys
> Are sung – but never more beautiful than there under the
> gun's noise.

I'd give a good deal to know what those roguish words were. Bawdy, I suppose, but just possibly 'red' words, which would give point to the 'human hopeful things' Gurney is introduced to in the Welsh pit boys' company.

In the second, and much longer, poem to carry the title 'First Time In', Gurney recalls the same incident, the meeting with the Welsh boys, the comradeship.

> What an evening! What a first time, what a shock
> So rare of home-pleasure beyond measure
> And always to time's ending surely a treasure.

These lines seem to bring the poem to a close, but then comes an asterisk followed by a further ten lines which act as a coda.

Kavanagh suggests the ten lines were 'presumably added later' (Kavanagh, 233) This, though, need not be the case. Parker, who has studied the manuscript carefully, claims that the asterisk shouldn't be there, and that the poem's final lines, far from being an afterthought, are crucially important to the poem's meaning. The poem has, indeed, been leading to them.

They begin:

> Since after-war so surely hurt, disappointed men
> Who looked for the golden Age to come friendly again.
> With inn evenings of meetings in warm glows,
> Talk; coal and wood fire uttering rosy shows
> With beer and 'Widdicombe Fair' ...

The Welshmen are, it will be seen, accepted as part of Gurney's imagined 'home-pleasure'. They are in no sense foreign or distant from him. Their hurt is therefore *his* hurt. Read inattentively and you may think he speaks of those he's earlier called 'the heroes of the story' as being 'sorely hurt'. But no, the phrase is 'surely hurt.' The phrase looks in two directions. The men *must* have been hurt. The hurt was *bound* to happen. The Golden Age *wasn't* to come again. In other words, the poem celebrates the worth of that glimpsed commonalty of men Gurney experienced in the trenches and at the same time mourns the fact that post-war England is as far removed as ever from the vision of a transformed society which had sustained soldiers in the trenches. 'North Woolwich' identified with 'Hellene memories', but in radical thought of the period the 'Golden Age' was more often linked to the moment Tawney placed in the latter half of the sixteenth century, between what he calls 'the meaninglessness of a feudalism gone senile ... and the demure austerities of the first, pious phase of capitalism'. That was where Gurney placed it, too. Hence his sonnet 'The Golden Age', which Kavanagh dates to the period 28 September – 21 December, 1922, when Gurney was in Barnwood House, a private asylum near Gloucester. There is nothing of madness about the sonnet, however, and especially not the sestet:

> O for some force to swing us back there to some
> Natural moving towards life's love, or that glow
> In the word to be glow in the State, that golden age come
> Again, men working freely as nature might show,

And a people honouring stage-scenes lit bright with fine sound
On a free soil, England happy, honoured and joy-crowned.

Whatever that force might be – revolutionary energy, and why not? – Gurney plainly yearns for a glow in the state not to be found in contemporary England. Whether he is writing about Welsh pit boys or the boys of Canning Town, certain of the poems written after 1920 absorb and/or transmit a feeling of betrayal. The certain hopes of the trenches, hopes that found expression not merely there but in wider contexts, have, for the moment at least, been denied. The Duke of Bilgewater and other English Prussians have survived. As a result, the soil still isn't free. Gurney is made to feel an exile in his own land.

III

It is this sense of exile, of being denied common ownership, which explains Gurney's intense, almost anguished, desire to *claim* the Cotswolds, his 'two-thousand year home', as he calls it. 'Nobody can't stop 'ee, it's / A footpath, right enough', Lob tells Edward Thomas, as the poet travels in Wiltshire 'In search of something chance would never bring'. Gurney pounds the footpaths and lanes of Gloucestershire and surrounding counties, eating up the miles, searching for – but, for what exactly? For a history, certainly, one he finds all about him. It is there as a matter of 'Generations' (one of two poems in *80 Poems or So* to bear the same title):

> There are runners yet on Cotswold,
> Though Will Squele he lies low,
> And men sow wheat on headlands
> That other men see grow.

> Eyes close and copper weights them,
> Babes as blind come to birth;
> Though John Gaunt's bets are ended
> And shallow Shallow's mirth.

Walter prints 'mummers' for 'runners', but 'runners' makes good sense, because in Act 3, scene 2, of *Henry IV Part Two* Justice Shallow is talking of his and his friends' exploits, which include boosting their physical prowess. The poem is subtler than may at first seem to be the case. It by no means wants to endorse an uncritical sense of continuity. Those babes 'as blind' as dead men will, after all, replace the garrulous and tricky John of Gaunt (Gurney wouldn't have shared the view, aired by Tories in the 1980s, that Shakespeare's dodgy customer 'spoke for England'). They will also replace the equally garrulous Justice Shallow, who happily allowed Falstaff to 'prick' hapless men for a battle in which they would almost certainly end up dead or mutilated. Why, General Haig was himself once a blind babe.

Moreover, the Cotswolds bear evidence of war's all-encompassing effects. Hence, 'Possessions' (again, one of two poems with identical titles, both to be found in Kavanagh):

> Sand has the ants, clay ferny weeds for play
> But what shall please the wind now the trees are away
> War took on Witcombe steep?
> It breathes there, and wonders at old night roarings;
> October time at all lights, and the new clearings
> For memory are like to weep.
> It was right for the beeches to stand over Witcombe reaches,
> Until the wind roared and softened and died to sleep.

This sense of a lost voice, a lost relationship, is keenly reminiscent of the opening of Clare's great poem 'To A Fallen Elm': 'Old elm that murmured in our chimney top / The sweetest anthem autumn ever made'. There, the word murmur evokes that posture of the human voice in close, loving relationship, just as the wind in Gurney's poem 'roared and softened and died to sleep'. Almost like a comical locally known sot, blustering into exhaustion.

But what is most intriguing about this deftly crafted little poem, with its subtle mix of masculine and feminine rhymes, of flexible line-lengths varying between three and six stresses, is that word 'right'. In what sense was it 'right for the beeches to stand over Witcombe reaches'? In the sense, we have surely to say, that it was natural. Natural right is what free-born Englishmen traditionally appeal to, but such right is endlessly contested, and often overthrown, by legally enforced acts. Acts of enclosure infamously took away land rights. In removing the trees from Witcombe steep, war has not merely created a breach in nature, it has silenced a collective voice, a presence, a throng.

A number of Gurney's poems at this time brood over the

misfortunes of change. There is natural, seasonal, change, as in 'Leckhampton Chimney Has Fallen Down', or as in 'The Change' itself, which draws on a Keatsian awareness of 'Summer's last challenge toward winter's merciless/Cohort', and the defiant sound of 'music, voice or violin's/Denial passionate of the frozen time'. Here, outer and inner weather become elided, and music offers release which in other, darker, lyrics seems unavailable. I think, for example, of 'When I am Covered', whose last three-line stanza runs

> Better to lie and be forgotten aye.
> In death his rose-leaves never is a crease.
> Rest squares reckonings Love set awry.

Whether this is human love, I don't know. The poem is similar to 'Moments', in which Gurney registers the 'loathed minutes' bringing him nearer to

> That six-foot-length I must lie in
> Sodden with mud, and not grieve again
> Because high Autumn goes beyond my pen
> And snow lies inexprest in the deep lane.

That last, extraordinary, line testifies to what lies at the heart of much of Gurney's poetry during this period. He is both celebrant and memorialist of a loved place that, without his unique vision, will not be seen by or become articulate to future generations. Lacking his words, the place will not be able to utter itself. Such anguished realization is, I suspect, compounded by Gurney's acute sense that the loved place, sealed as a perfect image in his mind for the time he was in France, now reveals itself as something rather different. The outer and inner weathers have changed.

He wasn't alone in sensing this. Thousands of men who returned from the trenches to post-war England must have experienced such anguish. They fought for a vision of England most often promoted as essentially pastoral, the great, good, smiling land of plenty, of peace, of love. They returned to an England that simply couldn't be sustained in such terms. Not surprisingly, they interpreted the cold reality as ingratitude. Very often, no doubt, there *was* ingratitude, not least in the unemployment they faced, the mean houses they had to go back to or which they were given, the scanting of their traumatic experiences. The war-time vows of government were followed by the shabby compromises of peace. Those who had promised them honour (or jobs) turned official scorn and sometimes tanks on them when they complained of being abandoned and tried to act in their own interests. That is inexcusable.

But it's more understandable, and so excusable, that those ordinary citizens – mostly women and children – who hadn't fought, and yet many of whom had been seduced by images of heroic, uncomplaining soldiers, warring nobly for a holy cause, should have little comprehension of what the actuality of war had been. The worlds of Severn and Somme, for all their alliterative chime, sound not so much connection as utter dislocation. No one who has heard family stories of the great-grandfather or uncle, or more distant relative, who returned from the front and who then walled themselves into silences broken only by sudden, inarticulate rages, can have any doubt of the cost of the men's war-time experience. Nor do I find it surprising that the children of such men should so often have feared their fathers, seen them as hostile and sometimes terrible strangers, and have been relieved at their not infrequent early deaths, deaths which tell of despair, of an utter hopelessness.

No other poet has spoken with such grieving, angry eloquence about the after-effects of war on the soldiers themselves as has Gurney.

MIST ON MEADOWS

Mist lies heavy on English meadows
As ever on Ypres, but the friendliness
Here is greater in full field and hedge shadows,
And there is less menace and no dreadfulness
As when the Verey lights went up to show the land stark.
Dreadful green light baring the ruined trees,
Stakes, pools, lostness, better hidden dreadful in dark
And not ever reminding of these other fields
Where tall dock and clover is, and this sweet grass yields
For that poisoned, where the cattle hoof makes mark,
And the river mist drifts slowly along the leas.

*

But they honour not – and salute not those boys who saw a terror
Of waste, endured horror, and were not fearer
Before the barrages like Heaven's anger wanton known –

Feared not and saw great earth spouts in terror thrown,
But could not guess, but could not guess, alas!
How England should take as common their vast endurance
And let them be but boys having served time overseas.

I quote the version to be found in Kavanagh. Walter's
Everyman also prints the first section, but not the surely crucial
lines that come after the break, and which entirely alter the
poem's meaning. The first section points the absolute contrast
between the hell that war has made of the French landscape,
and the English landscape where mist isn't formed of cordite,
poison gas, or the smoke of battle, and where the only
indentations in the soil come from the heavy tread of cattle.
('What passing-bells for those who die as cattle?' But it's next to
impossible that Gurney could have known Owen's sonnet.)

The last line of the opening section, with its linked vowel
sounds, *river, mist, drifts*, and the Tennysonian drag of 'slowly
along', seems to embody a perfection of langorous, pastoral
ease. This being so, it's important that such tranquil content-
ment should be broken by the very different mood of the second
section, poised as that is between regret and anger at how
'England should take as common [the] vast endurance' of those
who fought overseas. 'Common' is perhaps an unguarded word
here. After all, the soldiers' experience *was* common, in the sense
that it was commonly shared by all who fought. But Gurney
means that those who stayed behind or had no experience of
war chose to have no conception of how heroic was that vast
endurance. In which case it may be proper to recall the lines
from 'Insensibility' where Owen breathes a curse on 'dullards
whom no cannon stuns... /By choice they made themselves
immune/To pity and whatever moans in man'.

Given his acute sense of feeling unwelcome in his own land,
it's not to be wondered at that Gurney should occasionally
sound merely peevish in his rejection of changes. In the two
stanza poem of that title, he sounds for all the world like a
member of the Countryside Alliance in his grousing at those
who've shoe-horned their way into 'cottage' living.

> Peasants and willow pattern went together,
> And whiskers with the white road suited well.
> Now there's a mixtured hotch-potch hard to tell,
> 'Twill lame the mare, turn cream, and spoil the weather.

A similar note can be heard in 'The Bargain', a poem intended for the never published collection *Rewards of Wonder*. Here, Gurney writes of the loss of local history. A field called by locals 'Waltheof's Field', and replete with a knowable history

> will become a rubbish heap.
> Villas will stand there and look polite; with folk polite
> Where sedges stood for the wind's play and poet-delight,
> But Severn will be sorry and it can never be right.

Politeness is the antithesis of that playful, even erotically tinged 'wind's play'. And here, change registered as loss is not merely a sigh for past simplicities, but regret for new identities, tame proprieties. No use looking to the polite to make any change that matters. Once again, a natural 'right' has been ignored or cancelled.

IV

Faced with change, and therefore the imminent loss of a known history, Gurney becomes the memorialist of his 'native land'. There's nothing of the hand-wringing mode of lament for the 'immemorial past' with which such an enterprise has been all too easily infested in writing of the past two centuries. Gurney is, on the contrary, keenly aware of an imbricated history. Read aright, the Cotswolds reveal themselves as palimpsest. Hence, 'Cotswold Ways', which begins:

> One comes across the strangest things in walks:
> Fragments of Abbey tithe-barns fixed in modern
> And Dutch-sort houses where the water baulks
> Weired up, and brick kilns broken among fern,
> Old troughs, great stone cisterns bishops might have blessed
> Ceremonially, and worthy mounting-stones;
> Black timber in red brick, queerly placed
> Where Hill stone was looked for – and a manor's bones
> Spied in the frame of some wisteria'd house
> And mill-falls and sedge pools and Saxon faces;
> Stream-sources happened upon in unlikely places,
> And Roman-looking hills of small degree...

There are another three lines before the sentence finally stops. 'Cotswold Ways' unwinds as byways and lanes unwind. The poem refuses to order the 'strangest things': history isn't to be ticketed and badged, and this seemingly endless registering of different epochs and modes is, it should go without saying, generously inclusive. It testifies to the absurdity of claiming any one moment or tradition as quintessentially 'English'.

Nevertheless, Cotswold's Roman inheritance clearly counts for much in Gurney's account of that area of England so deeply embedded in his imagination. 'The Bare Line of the Hill' begins:

> The bare line of the hill
> Shows Roman and
> A sense of Rome hangs still
> Over the land.

It ends, nine stanzas later, with Gurney invoking 'The regal and austere/Mantle of Rome' thrown

> As of old – about the walls
> Of hills and the farm – the fields.
> Scabious guards the steeps,
> Trefoil the slopes yield.

In an almost Marvellian fancy, the native flora is seen as an army, part resistant (scabious), although on the lower ground – the slopes – trefoil yields to those who presumably pick it. But giving up also implies bounty. Gurney, passionate admirer of Thomas and especially of 'Lob', that compendium of local names for English wayside flowers, might have been expected to give the local names for both scabious and trefoil: 'bachelor's buttons' for the former, and for trefoil, and depending on whether he intends white clover (*Trifolium repens*), hop trefoil (*Trifolium campestre*) or birdsfoot trefoil (*Lotus corniculatus*), such names as 'claver', 'hop-clover', or 'butter-and-eggs', 'crowfeet', 'eggs-and-bacon', 'hen-and-chickens', 'pattens-and-clogs' or 'shoes-and-stockings'. The fact he *doesn't* is not to be taken to indicate he didn't know some at least of these local names, because he most certainly did. The opening of 'Hedges' runs: '"Bread and cheese" grow wild in the green time,/Children laugh and pick it'. Gurney almost certainly has in mind wood-sorrel, from the flowers of which, as Geoffrey Grigson remarks in his wondrous *The Englishman's Flora*, 'Generations of children have bitten the sharp, pleasant taste'. But the flower that yields to them could be birdsfoot trefoil.

If we want an explanation as to why in 'The Bare Line of the Hill' Gurney doesn't follow Thomas's example, we need only turn to the Introduction Marion Scott wrote for the account of Herbert Howells's music which appeared in *The Music Bulletin*, VI, May, 1924. Howells, she commented,

> Came naturally into an inheritance of beauty. Hill, sky, cloud, river – all these things are Gloucestershire, and behind them one glimpses the succession of centuries flowing down from the mists of time in an almost unruffled and ever-widening tide. Many races mingled their strains in the making of England. And there seems reason to believe that the Romans left here a deeper mark, one less obliterated by subsequent events than in most places elsewhere. Does any sign remain today of that Second Legion, proudly named Augustan (Royal), which occupied Gloucester for so long and watched the Marches of Wales? Who knows? It is a strange coincidence that two learned authorities on ethnography – quite unknown to each other – singled out Howells and his brothers as perfect types of Italian Celts.

My guess is that Scott derived from Gurney her reasons to believe in the Romans' deep mark on Gloucestershire. Gurney returned to the subject in 'Scabious and Trefoil', included in *Best Poems*, where he links the plants to 'the cohorts who guarded' high Cotswold. 'Trefoil thats nobler than the steely sword./ Scabious more Roman than the page of ordered/Sound like set metal.' There will be more to say about this, and of Gurney's Roman preoccupations, in the next chapter. Here, I will merely note that his sense of a complex English history is politically important precisely because it does its best to reject that little-England mentality which, like ground-elder, creeps endlessly through the subsoil of English life and which, for all the attempts to dig it out, is almost impossible to get rid of. It certainly flourished in the period that came immediately after the Great War, when instant heroes – none of whom had actually fought – proclaimed an England triumphant against all forms of foreign contamination, including, of course, bolshevism. There is no space here to follow through this new- or re-found insistence on 'essential' Englishness, but there is no doubt that it stank in the nostrils of those who had fought, survived, and who had now to find strategies for combating it. (See the note at the end of this chapter, p. 67.) The Gurney who wrote 'The Bare Line of the Hill' was a very different poet from the one who had written the 1917 'Sonnets for England'.

Yet his delight in what, in a different context, Randall Jarrell called 'the dailiness of life', in common things, was unfazed. Indeed, a poem to which Kavanagh gives the title 'The Dearness of Common Things' (in the Everyman and *80 Poems or So* the same poem appears under the more severe 'Common Things') seems not much more than a list of, among much else,

> Beech wood, tea, plate shelves,
> And the whole family of crockery,
> Woodaxes, blades, helves.
>
> Ivory milk, earth's coffee,
> The white face of books
> And the touch, feel, smell of paper,
> Latin's lovely looks....
>
> Wool, rope, cloth, old pipes
> Gone warped in service;
> And the one herb of tobacco,
> The herb of grace, the censer weed,
> Of whorled, blue, finger-traced curves.

Not everyone would think to include Latin in a list of loved common things. That Gurney does at least indicates his assumption that he doesn't see himself as belonging to an exclusive caste of learned men. And his rejoicing in tobacco and tea (which, as many poems including different versions of 'Tobacco' make clear – see, for example, Everyman, p. 31, and Kavanagh, p. 61 – have an almost sacramental quality for him) and 'earth's coffee' – I suppose he means its colour, although I wonder whether he might not have in mind the coffee made from acorns – is evidence of his identification with Thomas's use of the phrase 'common things'. As Stan Smith has well remarked, the phrase in Thomas's writing suffuses 'the merely commonplace with an exalted sense of the commonalty of experience and of things seen and held in common'.[8] But for Gurney 'The Dearness' of common things also attends to their non-utilitarian value. They are held dear, not because of their exclusivity, nor because their monetary value makes them objects of rarity, not dear in *that* sense, but dear precisely because they are *common*.

They are also, of course, associated with a world of work, or anyway a world that, in view of Latin's lovely looks being accorded no higher status than 'Woodaxes, blades, helves', testifies to the 'actual troublous life of every day, with toil of hands and brain together', the championing of which, to repeat, Edward Thomas so admired in William Morris. Hence, as we have seen, Gurney's poems celebrating everyday labour. There is also 'Felling a Tree', his wonderful account of the toil and pleasure, 'The surge of spirit that goes with using the axe'. The poem ends with his musing on how the felled tree 'tomorrow would be fuel for the bright kitchen for brown tea, against cold night'. The tree warms the household gods, those hospitable presences of the kitchen hearth.

But the poem which most wonderfully celebrates work and, with it, a life of absorption, of knowledge that in one sense is common, in another rare (because, even at the time when Gurney was writing his poem, it was becoming what we might call marginalized), is 'The Lock-Keeper'. This at least is the title given to the version of the poem to be found in *War's Embers*, where, underneath the title, Gurney adds '(To the Memory of Edward Thomas)'. The poem, which there is twenty-one lines long, offers an affectionate tribute to the kind of countryman we might expect to find in a good deal of Georgian poetry. It's not bad, but, if you except the Gurney signature revealed in occasional corrugations of rhythm and phrase, 'The Lock-Keeper' could have been written by any of a number of his contemporaries. It ends, conventionally enough, with Gurney paying tribute to the keeper's uniqueness in a manner that comes dangerously close to offering him as 'an unforgettable character'.

> I'll travel for many a year, nor ever find
> A winter-night companion more to my mind,
> Nor one more wise in ways of Severn river,
> Though her villages I search for ever and ever.

Not to put too fine a point on it, this is fustian.

But the poem Kavanagh prints is a very different matter. Shorn of its dedication, though nearly five times as long as the version that appeared in *War's Embers*, 'The Lock Keeper', as it is now called, belongs with Gurney's great work. Internal evidence suggests that the poem must have been written sometime in the summer of 1922, when his mental state was becoming markedly more troubling, to himself as to others. This will explain why, early in the poem, he speaks of the Lock Keeper as a man 'who goes in my dark mind', and later says 'It would have needed one far less sick than I / To have questioned, to have pried each vein of his wide lore'. Moreover, there are enough signs of discontinuity and needless repetition in the poem to suggest that what we have is work Gurney left in an unfinished or unresolved state. Blunden, Clark and Hurd all print the poem, but they and Kavanagh are forced to work from a manuscript, as the poem was never published in Gurney's lifetime. Indeed he seems not to have intended it for any particular collection of those many he put together or planned.

If I nevertheless want to press the case for considering 'The Lock Keeper' as among his major work it's because it gathers up many of his abiding concerns in a manner that is passionate, articulate, and deeply compelling. 'The Lock-Keeper' begins, without fuss or preamble, 'A tall lean man he was, proud of his gun'. In the later version this becomes:

> Men delight to praise men; and to edge
> A little further off from death the memory
> Of any noted or bright personality
> Is still a luck and a poet's privilege.
> And so the man who goes in my dark mind
> With sand and broad waters and general kind
> Of fish-and-fox-and-bird lore, and walking lank;
> Knowledge of net and rod and rib and shank,
> Might well stretch out my mind to be a frame –
> A picture of a worthy without name.

It's significant that Gurney almost casually introduces reference to his own 'dark mind'. The confident generalization of the opening lines speaks, not of the poet's uniqueness, but of his 'luck' and 'privilege' in being able to praise 'any noted or bright personality'. This latter phrase in particular looks at first to be a cliché, but is redeemed from that not merely by the contrast it points with the poet's own 'dark mind', lit up as that is by memory of the Lock Keeper, but by the images of light that accompany the keeper through the poem, of eyes 'gone flaming on work', of his shape by the chimney-corner, 'Shadow and bright flare', of his association with 'firelight and lamplight'.

The keeper flares with intense life, or, as Gurney says, 'bright life'.

'Let us now praise famous men.' The injunction is directed towards heroes, military men, men of public affairs. But Gurney won't even give a name to the man whose portrait his mind expands to contain. The Lock Keeper is any man. Or rather, his identity is knowable through work, through his total absorption in a life which the poet can scarcely grasp and to which he feels markedly inferior. 'There was nothing he did not know; there was nothing, nothing'. This line comes after a section detailing the Lock Keeper's understanding of animal ways, of what is usually called 'country lore', and which Gurney presents as 'knowledge transcending/Books, from long vain searches of dull fact'. For Gurney, himself, he says, 'more used to book-poring than bright life', the keeper acquires an almost heroic status.

There is of course a distinctive trait among writers of the modern period to praise the active man at the expense of the writer's own sedentary life, of a life, as Yeats put it, 'grown sluggish and contemplative'. There is similarly a recognizable preference among those who resist the soft snares of bourgeois existence for a life of defiant and, as it is usually perceived, joyous marginality. Tramps, beggars, gypsies, feature as almost mythic figures, embodiments – or at least tokens – of regenerative power, in the work of such otherwise different writers as Forster, Yeats, Lawrence and Edward Thomas. Such figures, even at their most mythic, can help focus the proper anxieties, dissatisfactions and discontents of modern living. But they can also become mere cardboard cut-outs – another emblem there. What saves Gurney's anonymous Lock Keeper from such a fate is the distance the poet keeps from a man who remains mysterious. Gurney doesn't pretend entirely to understand or share in his knowledge, though he certainly pays tribute to his intelligence. The keeper isn't, in other words, patronized as a figure of 'instinctive' or 'intuitive' wisdom. He has 'A net of craft of eye, heart, kenning and hand./Thousand-threaded tentaculous intellect/Not easy on a new thing to be wrecked.' Among the definitions the *OED* provides of 'kenning' are 'Teaching, instruction. Mental cognition; knowledge, understanding, awareness, recognition'. The dictionary also remarks that the word is 'Now *Sc.* [Scottish] *& North'*. I've no idea whether 'kenning' was much heard in the Cotswolds during the early part of the twentieth century. Probably not. That Gurney should nevertheless apply the word to his Lock Keeper must surely be because he wants to imply the man's unusual qualities, ones that aren't to be trapped in conventional terms. This is praise indeed.

Occasionally it veers towards the hagiographic. Contrasting his own sickness with the keeper's 'wide lore', Gurney says:

> One should be stable, and be able for wide views,
> Have knowledge, and skilled manage of questions use
> When the captain is met, the capable in use,
> The pictured mind, the skilled one, the hawk-eyed one;
> The deft-handed, quick-moving, the touch-commanded one.

The Lock Keeper as captain of Gurney's soul. At this instant the keeper becomes almost an impossible amalgam of accomplishments. And indeed at the end of the poem Gurney actually suggests that the keeper offered him 'Revelations; a time of learning and little said / On my part, since the Master he was so wise'. The Lock Keeper, even more than the Hedger, is thus a figure of veneration. But he is so for the very good reason that what another writer might have called his 'fullness of being' acts both as proof of the value of a life lived beyond utilitarian consideration and as rebuke to the assumption that those who are conventionally well-educated are superior human beings. For the Lock Keeper, who is friendly with 'coalmen, farmers, fishermen', there is 'talk with equals'. The intense heart of Gurney's poem affirms a democratic vision, one moreover that brings into the present – just – a similar vision to that which 'First Time In' mourned for, left, as it there seemed, in the trenches of war-time France.

NOTE: 'ENGLISHNESS' IN THE 1920s

In my book *The Radical Twenties*, I have pointed out how education was recruited at the outset of the decade as a means of instilling in children a sense of their 'Englishness', and that this entailed inculcating a 'national pride in the language as well as the literature'. Naturally, the version of that language on which pride could repose was 'standard English'. Naturally, too, such language would be the glue to stick together the different social classes.[9] At the same time, England was, in Stanley Baldwin's phrase, 'the country'. And Baldwin, prime minister for much of the 1920s, saw the country as quintessentially 'English' in so far as it maintained 'tradition'. In other words, Baldwin's vision of the country is deeply conservative and reactionary.

3

The Later Years

SONNET. SEPTEMBER 1922

Fierce indignation is best understood by those
Who have time or no fear, or a hope in its real good
One loses it with a filed soul or in sentimental mood
Anger is gone with sunset, or flows as flows
The water in easy mill-runs; the earth that ploughs
Forgets protestation in its turning, the rood
Prepares, considers, fulfils, and the poppy's blood
Makes old the old changing of the headlands brows.

But the toad under the harrow toadiness
Is known to forget, and even the butterfly
Has doubts of wisdom when that clanking thing goes by
And's not distressed. A twisted thing keeps still
That thing easier twisted than a grocers bill
And no history of November keeps the guy.

This remarkable sonnet must have been written at the moment
when Gurney's erratic behaviour was causing great concern,
especially to his newly married brother Ronald, into whose
house Gurney moved uninvited in September 1922. While there,
Michael Hurd tells us, he 'would shut himself in the front
room...and shout for them to keep away. He would sit with a
cushion on his head to guard against electric waves coming
from the wireless....He sneered at his brother's orthodoxies:
"Only fools go to work – why don't you get someone else to
keep you."... He threatened suicide and called at the police
station to demand a revolver.' Not surprisingly, Ronald couldn't
cope. Gurney was moved first to a convalescent home near
Bristol and then, after two doctors had certified him as insane, to

Barnwood House, a private asylum near Gloucester, which he entered on 28 September. He made two attempts to escape from Barnwood House, although on both occasions he was quickly recaptured, the second time when he walked into a police station, perhaps to repeat his demand for a revolver. Finally, on 21 December 1922, he was transferred to the City of London Mental Hospital at Dartford, where he was to spend the rest of his life.

There is no point in denying that at this time Gurney was in a dreadfully disturbed state of mind, a danger to himself and damnably unpleasant to others. On the other hand, 'Sonnet. September 1922' cannot be explained away as the incoherent ravings of an incurably sick man. For all its difficulties – and it is a very dense, impacted poem – it makes sense, and the sense it makes is crucial to an understanding of Gurney's work. In the first place, we need to recognize that 'Fierce indignation' isn't to be traced back to Gurney's own inability to find regular employment, nor to his feeling that, as Hurd puts it, 'he had been betrayed by the country he loved and whose cause his art and life had served. Were the sufferings of a war poet to count as nothing... Was there to be no reward for all the pain he had endured?' Such indignation, genuine though it is, abuts on self-pity. But in Gurney's sonnet, those who burn with 'fierce indignation' live in hope of its being of use. They imagine 'its real good'. 'Those/Who have time or no fear' are therefore very different from 'One' who loses indignation 'with a filed soul or in sentimental mood'. Gurney opposes the group to the individual, whose soul is defiled or has been filed down – its rough edges smoothed away – or who has become part of the rank and file, of those who accept their lot. (This may explain if it doesn't entirely excuse Gurney's sneers 'at his brother's orthodoxies'.) The rest of the octave is about acceptance, even the acceptance of sacrifice, whether that's the crucifixion of Christ or the slaughter of soldiers, which is surely implied in the poppy's blood: it's as though each season poppies worn on the headland's brows act as reminder of a new supply of soldiers springing up only to be mown down.

The sestet, however, brings a change signalled by the opening word, 'But'. Even toad and butterfly may learn to be other than submissive or ready to live for the day alone. The plough which threatens them and which is surely here presented as the apparent juggernaut of history, of what happens to happen, can be opposed. But then, in the poem's final turn, we learn that such opposition can't be expected of those who have been so 'twisted' by events that they are like paper spills, the hapless means to others' ends and for which they, too, are sacrificed, cancelled from history.

My reading of this extraordinary poem is to some extent speculative, but of one thing I am certain: that 'Sonnet. September 1922' is not the work of a madman, though it is undoubtedly the work of a poet sorely perplexed and angered by the times in which he finds himself. The perplexity and anger are, it's true, occasionally turned to his own special condition, as in 'To God', which may have been the first poem he wrote in Barnwood, and where he asks, 'Why have you made life so intolerable / And set me within four walls'; but again the poem is perfectly lucid. It may be about a sense of near-impotent despair, but it possesses the sanity of true art.

The same can be said about 'A wish', a very fine poem which Gurney must have written soon after his move to Dartford. It begins:

> I would wish for the children of West Ham
> Wooden-frame houses, square with some-sort stuff
> Crammed in to keep the wind away that's rough,
> And rain, in summer cool, in cold comfortable enough.
> Easily destroyed – and pretty enough, and yet tough
> Instead of brick and mortar tiled houses of no
> Special appearance or attractive show.

He goes on to wish that such houses shouldn't be crowded together and should have plots of land for working, because these will keep out of harm

> The mind that's always good when let go its way
> (I think) so there's work enough in a happy day.

That characteristic run-over is here given an extra jolt by our realization that, writing from the asylum, Gurney's note of caution is a kind of appeal for freedom to work.

In work is sanity. The poem is greatly sane in its plea for good, cheap housing for the poor. Which means abandoning bricks and mortar, notorious for their unhealthy retention of cold and damp. In the immediate post-war years there was a need for a massive house-building programme, though precious little was achieved and most of what went on involved profiteering and jerry-built constructions of the worst kind. In the face of this shoddy exploitation, architects such as the utopian socialist Clough Williams Ellis argued for the need to do away with bricks and mortar, and throughout the 1920s there were repeated attempts to find alternatives. To take two examples: The *Illustrated London News* for 2 August 1924 ran a feature on 'Durocrete' – a mixture of wood and concrete, which, it said, could be used to solve the housing shortage because such a synthetic material was easy to manufacture. Four years later, the annual Ideal Home Exhibition, sponsored by the *Daily Mail*, trumpeted a 'House of the Future' built of 'a horn-like substance' cut as sheets. (It sounds rather like Bakelite.)

I mention these matters because they help to explain why Gurney should conclude 'A wish' with the following:

> O better this sort of shelter –
> And villages on the land set helter-skelter
> On hillsides, dotted on plains; than* the too exact
> Straight streets of modern times that straight and strict
> And formal keep man's spirit within bounds,
> Where too dull duties keep in monotonous rounds
>
> These villages to make for these towns of today –
> O Haste – and England shall be happy with the May
> Or meadow-reach to watch, miles to see and away.

I. B. Gurney
Stone House, Dartford, Kent (Appealing for Death or Release.)

Anyone who can offer such sensible advice deserves to be released into a useful life. Either that, or he may as well be dead.

Reading 'A wish', I think of the American poet Hart Crane's insistence that modern poetry must learn to absorb the machine if it is to be truly modern. Hart Crane was announcing this at virtually the same moment as Gurney was writing his poem, and there's not much doubt in my mind as to who is more properly addressing the modern world. Not that I wish to score a cheap point against Hart Crane, a poet I admire. But while he does not lack for admirers – many of whom take for granted his

---

* Walter in the Everyman prints 'that' but Gurney must mean 'than', as Kavanagh prints in *Collected Poems*.

four-square modernity – Gurney is still hobbled by the assumption that he's somehow a late Georgian. Yet what Georgian poet wrote about housing conditions in London's East End, or, for that matter, offered good, practical advice on the best designs, building materials, and arrangement of houses for the poor? 'A wish' is not so much Georgian as Georgic. Applied Georgic, it's true, its wise practicality offered not for rural husbandry but urban living, but nevertheless true to the spirit of the original.

Gurney was locked away in Stone House, Dartford, when he wrote 'A wish'. The asylum, with its unvarying routines and prison-like atmosphere, must have felt the very embodiment of dull duties and monotonous rounds. When Helen Thomas visited Gurney there in the early 1930s, she was shocked by the hospital's oppressive, prison-like atmosphere. She recoiled from the bare corridors and Gurney's 'little cell-like bedroom where the only furniture was a bed and a chair. The window was barred and the walls were bare and drab... Before we left he took us into a large room in which was a piano and on this he played to us and the tragic circle of men who sat on hard benches against the walls of the room.' The whole place seems like one of Piranesi's visions of *I Carceri*.

Yet it would be quite wrong to think that 'A wish' is concerned, no matter how indirectly, with Gurney's own terrible predicament. Though his imagination may have been in some sense prompted by that, the poem is an entirely sane protest against outmoded and, more important, inefficient kinds of civic architecture, especially housing for the poor. Its Blake-like vision is of an England set free from the constraints of those modes of living which fetter the spirit and drive out the capacity for creative joy. And in this it very strikingly anticipates Lawrence's great essay of 1929, 'Nottingham and the Mining Country'. Here, Lawrence protests at the foulness of that industrial spirit which 'in the palmy Victorian days' condemned the workers

> to ugliness, ugliness, ugliness: meanness and formless and ugly surroundings, ugly ideals, ugly religion, ugly hope, ugly love... ugly relationship between workers and employers. The human soul needs actual beauty even more than bread...
>
> If the company, instead of building those sordid and hideous

Squares, then, when they had that lovely site to play with, there on the hill top: if they had put a tall column in the middle of the small market-place, and run three parts of a circle of arcade round the pleasant space, where people could stroll or sit, and with the handsome houses behind...[1]

Lawrence has in mind Eastwood, Gurney West Ham. Both, however, see the true spirit of work and play as expressions of creativity. It is 'the mind that's always good when let go its way', or what Lawrence in his essay calls the collier's 'peculiar sense of beauty, coming from his intuitive and instinctive consciousness'.[2]

I am not trying to force these two great, individual writers into a single mould. They are separated by more than the five years that come between Lawrence's birth in 1885 and Gurney's in 1890. But when Lawrence at the end of his essay implores his readers to 'Make a new England', he is voicing precisely that urgent desire for change which runs through Gurney's writing. And he would have understood, and I have no doubt approved of, 'The Escape', another poem that seems to belong to early 1923.

> I believe in the increasing of life whatever
> Leads to the seeing of small trifles...
> real, beautiful, is good, and an act never
> Is worthier than in freeing spirit that stifles
> Under ingratitude's weight; nor is anything done
> Wiselier than the moving or breaking to sight
> Of a thing hidden under by custom; revealed
> Fulfilled, used, (sound-fashioned) any way out to delight.
>   .   .   .   .
> Trefoil...hedge sparrow...the stars on the edge of night.

A 'spirit that stifles/Under ingratitude's weight'. Although that can certainly be understood as a reference to his own plight, 'The Escape' is no more to be explained away than are the vast majority of poems which Gurney wrote during the early years of his confinement. Not even the title has to be thought of as voicing his desire for freedom from Stone House. As Jeremy Hooker has noted, the poem is about redeeming vision from what Coleridge called 'the lethargy of custom', and the meanings contained within the phrase 'sound-fashioned' are therefore crucial. The most immediate meaning, soundly or well-made, is, Hooker notes, 'represented elsewhere by [Gurney's] emphasis on "square-making"'. And he adds that this connects with his 'feeling of the craftsman's hand and eye'. This then links to a second meaning: the 'craftsmanwise meaning of "sound-fashioned", drawing out its moral connotations, in the sense "made whole".'

How deeply Gurney believed in the craftsman's art can be seen in 'We Who Praise Poets', one of the *80 Poems or So*. Here, he identifies the craft of poetry with that of the master-carpenter, the mason and the house-builder:

> The crafted art, the smooth curve, and surety
> Come not of nature till the apprentice free
> Of trouble with his tools, and cobwebbed cuts,
> Spies out a path his own and casts his plots.
> Then, looking back on four-square edifices
> And wind-and-weather standing tall houses
> He stakes a court and tries his unpaid hand...

'Four-square' here becomes 'square-making' in 'Compensations', which phrase is repeated in yet another of the *80 Poems or So*, where Gurney speaks of the love of 'Making four-square' ('Polite Request'). And without stretching a point too far, it's legitimate to note how much terse energy Gurney gains for the phrase 'Spies out a path his own' by cutting out the word 'of', as a mason might knock away a lump of unnecessary mortar.

The third meaning of 'sound-fashioned' is to be expected of Gurney the musician. Again, Hooker puts the matter very well when he notes that fashioning from sound is one of Gurney's greatest gifts.

> The reality of his places owes much to his acute sensitivity to weathers, effects of light, movements, physical sensations. These impressions of a world vividly alive and intensely experienced are rendered by his rhythms and syntax, his quick elliptical imagistic detail, and his mastery of patterns of verbal sound.[3]

Given the urgent impetus of Gurney's poetry at its most characteristic, 'four-square' may not seem an entirely appropriate term for how it's made or how we respond to it. This isn't to downgrade his occasional, exquisitely wrought lyrics, nor yet other forms such as the sonnet, or the four-line stanzas of 'Imitation', a poem only to be found in Kavanagh. In a note Kavanagh, who has studied the mss., tells us that Gurney 'appears to try rhythmical notation in lines 9–10: "...To a . smooth going/And . flowing..."', and the poem, to my ear, seems a most beautiful experiment in modulating rhythms:

> Cottagers are happier now
> Than any perhaps
> Of the townsfolk, tired
> Decent at hours' lapse.

That was written in pre-asylum days. Not surprisingly, such lyrics aren't to be looked for in the Dartford years. As he said in 'Old Times', the happiness of freedom, of 'A four hours' tramping' is 'all gone now'. And, for Gurney, freedom is inseparable from the desire for work, *not* that laborious, mind-numbing toil which he rightly sees as dull duties kept in monotonous rounds, but such work as he celebrates in 'The Mangel-bury', a poem he wrote sometime between early 1925 and April 1926, and which is not merely deservedly well-known, but which shows how completely absurd it is to think of him as a mad poet.

> It was after War, Edward Thomas had fallen at Arras –
> I was walking by Gloucester musing on such things
> As fill his work with goodness; it was February; the long house
> Straw-thatched of the mangels stretched two wide wings;
> And looked as part of the earth heaped up by dead soldiers
> In the most fitting place – along the hedges yet-bare lines.
> West spring breathed there early, that none foreign divines.

This opening speaks both of loss and continuity, of a great dead poet and other dead soldiers and yet of a 'goodness', a quality of poetry for whose future Gurney now senses he must take responsibility. We know this to be so, because from musing on Thomas he is made suddenly aware of a 'straw-thatched' mangel clamp, like, it may be, 'the gable from the roof of clay/ On the long swede pile' of Thomas's poem 'Swedes'. It isn't, however, the recollection of individual poems that matters so much as Gurney's ardent – you could almost say desperate – identification with the 'goodness' which fills Thomas's poems. For Gurney, such goodness is imbued with an intimate know-ledge of place, 'that none foreign divines', and which is contained within the figure of the man who now appears, a farmer.

He was the thick-set sort of farmer, but well-built –
Perhaps long before, his blood's name ruled all:
Watched all things for his own. If my luck had so willed
Many questions of lordship I had heard him tell – old
Names, rumours. But my pain to more moving called
And him to some barn business far in the fifteen acre field.

Gurney is as careful as ever Thomas was not to appropriate a history. There is no question of his providing a genealogy for the farmer, still less of confidently setting him up as an archetypal English yeoman. For despite Gurney's willingness to help the farmer load his cart with mangels – 'we threw them with our bodies swinging; blood in my ears singing' – the poem concludes, not with some sententious bonding between the two men, but in a separation which makes clear the inevitable gap between them. They are differently called. In which case it matters hugely that Gurney does not end with himself, no matter how great the temptation to justify, even hypostasize, the Romantic figure of the poet summonsed by his pain to an apartness. Instead, he ends with the farmer himself, called to 'barn business'. And in so doing, the poet makes clear that the separation that exists between the two isn't evidence of his own superiority, any more than he feels superior to the Hedger. Farmer and hedger are both skilled workmen. (And traditionally, as every schoolboy in Gurney's day would have known, the farmer is an image of the poet, just as verse is linked to the ploughing of a furrow.)

'The Mangel-bury' and 'Hedger' were written in Dartford. Both poems are much taken up with Gurney's acute yearning to do useful work, and with his grieved sense of how absolute the gap is now between himself and those men of enviable skills with whom he tries to work. What never varies is his deep commitment to work itself. Hurd prints a long poem that belongs to the asylum years, which reads for all the world as an Apologia Pro Sua Vita, and which is headed

For the English Police
For Scotland Yard

Chance to Work

The poem runs to over 300 lines and is therefore far too long to quote, but anyone who cares about Gurney must hope that it will be reprinted in some future edition of his poems.

> I never had a chance to work, for when a boy
> Small day was mine, bed-time too soon came by –
> Few friends were mine who might have taught me books;
> Yet I loved Nature with its joyous looks;
> Played football hard as most, and the Cathedral
> Worshipped surely, with its great rise and fall.

So it begins, unremarkable perhaps apart from the opening phrase, which suggests that Gurney sees himself called on to give an explanation for his present predicament and is appealing to the police to free him so that he can work. The poem takes in his schooldays, his move to London and the Royal College of Music, his war years, his post-war experiences, his friendships, his love of Gloucester, of tea-drinking, of the Elizabethan writers 'Green, Dekker, and Marston – /Shirley, Massinger, Ford, and greater Jonson', of modern music. But running right through the poem is Gurney's desire for work, his belief in it, the occasional exultance at achieving it, whether it is 'wood hewing, labouring with spade./Hedging, plough-helping, stone shifting', or 'Working in strict discipline, music or strict rhyme'. Above all, the poem passionately reiterates his conviction that 'Labour was good'.

In the closing lines, Gurney pleads: 'Grant pity, grant chance of Work, Grant that/Freedom of effort in other days held to be great'. And there is the nub of the matter. Earlier in the poem he has vehemently claimed that his was 'a spirit that loved working'. He also says that 'the spirit forgives/Best in freedom', and still earlier has asked, 'Chance of work? Yes, but one hoped so in the coming/Peace, the hoped for universal true homing/Of Line and all Force'. It is the cancelling of these hopes, the defeat, as it must have seemed to him, of that widely shared vision of what in his early sonnet he had called 'the brotherhood of man' and which here becomes 'universal true homing/Of line and all Force' (turning swords into ploughshares), which he sees as putting out of reach a chance of free work. Of course, the poem is centred on himself. But it cannot be understood if we do not consider it in the context of other asylum poems. Above all, we shall not fully grasp the poem's bitter and anguished sanity if we fail to connect it to the many poems of the asylum years in which Gurney revisits his war experiences. And it is to these that we must now turn.

II

In his introduction to the *Collected Poems*, Kavanagh remarks that, during the asylum years, Gurney writes poems which inhabit the past, 'for as far as he is concerned, he has no present'. This is essentially true, as is Kavanagh's observation that, especially before 1926, Gurney produces so many entirely successful poems, and with such 'variety of tone and style', that they 'make one wonder why he was where he was'. Indeed. Then why *was* he immured in Stone House. Well, because he had been certified insane. George Walter identifies the particular nature of this insanity as schizophrenia, and in the lengthy introduction to his invaluable edition of *Rewards of Wonder* spends much time discovering clues to its existence in poetry written well before Gurney's incarceration.

> Recognising the subtlety with which the symptoms of Gurney's mental illness are inscribed in *Rewards of Wonder* means that it is necessary to look again at the practice of categorising his poetry as either 'pre-asylum' or 'asylum'. The use of these categories implies that it is possible to draw a line between two distinct phases in Gurney's development, one in which he was writing sanely and the other in which he was writing in the throes of madness. But once it is acknowledged that those qualities that mark *Rewards of Wonder* out as a schizophrenic text are present in all of Gurney's work – Blunden saw them as giving Gurney's poetry its 'peculiar unconventionality' and 'uncommon melody' . . . – then that distinction becomes meaningless. Everything that he wrote is characterised by cognitive processes which, in their most overt forms, are used to diagnose a recognised form of clinical insanity; how then is it possible to make a distinction between those of his poems which should be seen as 'sane' and those which should be seen as 'insane'? Gurney's certification in September 1922 is certainly a key moment biographically speaking, but the lifelong nature of his illness and the enduring impact that it had upon his creativity means that regarding his commital as some kind of turning-point in his artistic evolution creates a highly artificial picture of that evolution.

The problem with this is that, though it relies entirely on speculation as to the nature of Gurney's illness, it then turns speculation to certainty in order to explain away Gurney's poetry. To be fair to Walter, he occasionally tries to guard against this. Nevertheless, the effect of his approach is to reduce

Gurney's poems to evidence of a man in the grip of a mental illness he can do little to counter. Yet the poems so far considered in this chapter, and indeed in earlier chapters, are clear evidence of Gurney's success in producing free-standing work, and this applies as much to 'Hedger' and 'The Mangelbury', which date from well into the asylum period, as it does to 'The Hoe Scrapes Earth' or 'Felling a Tree', which precede it. Besides, to quote Blunden's praise of Gurney's *peculiar* unconventionality and *uncommon* conventionality as evidence of schizophrenic tendencies is at best to misunderstand the sense of Blunden's meaning. 'Peculiar' here doesn't mean 'weird' but 'distinct', for goodness' sake.

If the matter of Gurney's certification requires some discussion, the better approach is via Eric Leed's important study of *No Man's Land: Combat and Identity in World War I*. Towards the end of his book, Leed has a chapter entitled 'Exit from the Labyrinth: Neuroses and War' in which, in one section, he considers 'War Neurosis in Postwar Society'. Of such neurosis, or what he also calls Psychoneurotic diseases, Leed remarks that they proved for many survivors to be enduring. 'The pathologies generated by war continued to fill the wards of veterans' hospitals. But just as often these pathologies did not appear in the medical statistics, for they were worked out in offices, households, taverns, and the political arena'.[4] Anyone who has any aquaintance with those who fought in the Great War, either directly or through relatives, will understand the justice of Leed's remark. The war left permanent scars, mental as well as physical, on nearly all who fought in it. And for all anyone can know, Gurney was no more traumatized than many who continued to live at large – and often prove a torment to their immediate families, as he did to his. Indeed, Leed goes on to suggest that one reason for the mental discomfort of many soldiers who returned home after the war was their discovery (or realization) that the idealized image of home which had sustained them in the trenches could not survive the reality of day-to-day living. And this may well be why, as Leed notes, 'among veterans psychoses actually increased in absolute terms throughout the 1920s. More pensions for psychotic illnesses were granted by the British government in 1929 than had been granted in the four years immediately after the war.' In other words, war neurosis 'was a way-station on the road to a more fundamental break with reality'.[5]

All this is interesting and may be relevant to Gurney. But what really comes very close to him is Leed's account of the aggression felt by many returning soldiers towards their own societies. They had been fighting, as they supposed, for shared ideals, but they returned to nations which seemed not to care about those ideals, for whom, in fact, 'ideals' were at best a means to trick soldiers into fighting for a seemingly beyond-question cause. Leed invokes Philip Gibbs, who, he says, 'had hoped that the returning front soldiery would lead a movement for a national revitalisation in England', but who was now 'forced to recognise that the characteristic readiness for violence of the veteran was inherently apolitical, something that originated in a very deep psychic injury'. And he quotes Gibbs's own words on these returned veterans:

> they had not come back the same men. Something had altered them. They were subject to queer moods and queer tempers, fits of profound depression alternating with a restless desire for pleasure. Many were easily moved to passion where they lost control of themselves, many were bitter in their speech, violent in opinion, frightening.[6]

With this in mind, Gurney's outburst at his brother becomes entirely understandable. 'Only fools go to work – why don't you get somebody else to keep you.' In common with others, Gurney had, so he came to believe, fought for a world in which freedom to work would be guaranteed. Work, decent, *enlivening* work, would be an essential part of the transformed society he eagerly anticipated once war was done. Instead, the old were still in command, nothing had changed, the kind of work he cared about was denied to those thousands of returned soldiers who had to tramp from town to town, being careful to 'keep out of face how heart burns'. And now he himself had had freedom taken away from him. No wonder he wanted to go back to his war years. For *there*, in those shared trench experiences, were to be found the legitimate dreams of making a new world. In Leed's words:

> Capitalist society had not ceased being capitalist society by virtue of the war, in spite of the initial, overpowering sense of community.

This was the greatest disillusionment of many who believed that the war would bring with it a spiritual, communal transformation. In the trenches, and in numerous encounters with the home, it was shown that the economy of sacrifice and blood had been absorbed in the market of goods, capital, and labor.[7]

I'm not sure what Leed means by a spiritual transformation, but for the rest he's entirely accurate.

In their introduction to *80 Poems or So*, Thornton and Walter remark that Gurney's post-war poetry is marked by a new confidence and an expansion of themes, 'though it should first be remarked that there is a curious silence about the war'.[8] In fact, he wasn't entirely silent about the war, not even then. But it's understandable that in 1919 he should have felt the war was behind him and therefore done with. Ahead lay a future he and his companions had imagined and promised themselves and each other, and that they had been repeatedly promised as they endured the long, agonizing years of trench warfare. But if that was how matters seemed in the immediate post-war period, it didn't take long before they understood that the dreamed-of future was turning into a nightmare present, one moreover that seemed dismayingly like the discredited past. What was the *point* of all those deaths, that sacrifice the soldiers had been assured was glorious, that honour they had been told they upheld in combat, that duty which was supposedly sacred?

Perhaps such questions are always asked in time of war and even more after it is over and its human cost is becoming increasingly apparent. Somewhere in the background lurks Robert Southey's poem about the battle of Blenheim, with its puzzled, sardonic awareness of reputations won and lost, lives destroyed – and for what?

> 'And everybody praised the Duke
>   Who this great fight did win'.
> 'But what good ever came of it?'
>   Quoth little Peterkin.
> 'Why that I cannot tell,' said he,
> 'But 'twas a famous victory.'

Robert Browning, writing at the time of the Crimean War, is even more powerfully opposed to what he sees as militaristic vainglory. 'Love Among the Ruins', which stands at the head of

81

his great collection of 1855, *Men and Women*, surveys empires which might in one year send 'a million fighters forth', and begs Earth to 'Shut them in,/With their triumphs and their glories and the rest!/Love is best.' The catalogue of military achievement is contemptuously waved away: 'and the rest!' This is very close to Dickens's contemptuous dismissal of the claims made for Mr Edmund Sparkler, the lunk-head son of Mr Merdle, who in *Little Dorrit* is made a Lord of the Circumlocution Office, 'as a graceful and gracious mark of homage...and all the rest of it, with blast of trumpet'.

No such blast for the soldiers who march to war in Wilfred Owen's 'The Send-Off'.

> So secretly, like wrongs hushed-up, they went.
> They were not ours:
> We never heard to which front these were sent...
>
> Shall they return to beatings of great bells
> In wild train-loads?
> A few, a few, too few for drums and yells,
>
> May creep back, silent, to village wells,
> Up half-known roads.

Owen, who knew the real cost of war, understands what the future holds for those 'too few' soldiers who will return as though in disgrace – creeping into a semi-hidden existence, their wrongs forever hushed-up.

The pathos of men who march away to death or broken lives is most scarifyingly evoked by the American poet Randall Jarrell, in a poem which, while it may owe something to 'The Send-Off', seems to me a definitive statement of hopes betrayed, lies exposed.

A WAR

> There set out, slowly, for a Different World,
> At four, on winter mornings, different legs...
> You can't break eggs without making an omelette
> – That's what they tell the eggs.

By inverting the cliché, you can't make an omelette without breaking eggs – if you want something good it will cost you – Jarrell's mordant epigrammatic poem exposes the grandiose lies of those who claim to be making a new (Different) world. *We Are*

Making A New World is the title of one of the most famous paintings of the Great War, a ruined landscape by Paul Nash, over which a sun rises, or on which it sets, behind blood-red clouds that seem to have been sucked up out of the devastated earth, now and forever devoid of human presence. (The painting is on show at the Imperial War Museum.)

Nash's disenchantment with the war was, it hardly needs saying, widely shared. It came quickly to an American novelist-to-be who fought in Italy during the war's latter stages.

> 'Now, for a long time...I had seen nothing sacred and the things that were glorious had no glory and the sacrifices were like the stockyards at Chicago if nothing were done with the meat except to bury it. There were many words which you could not stand to hear and finally only the names of places had dignity.

That is Ernest Hemingway, in *A Farewell to Arms*. Speaking of the poems which make up *Rewards of Wonder*, George Walter says that the words ' "England", "war", "Rome", "Gloucester" and "poet" appear with monotonous frequency, as do references to Gurney's "right", his "wonder" and his need for "honour" in particular.' 'Glory', too, features in these poems, and we might assume that Gurney is trying to reclaim the worth of such a word, which Hemingway rightly considers to have been largely drained of meaning by the propagandist cant of officialdom, just as his repeated naming of French place names and of Cotswold villages and local features is a way of asserting their reality, their irreduceable presence to which history is attached. Walter cites all this as evidence of 'the process in schizoid thinking whereby a schizophrenic's attention becomes "trapped on one topic or word, rather as happens when a record becomes cracked." ' Put to this kind of a test, which poet would 'scape whipping? Wordsworth: 'nature', 'heart', 'man', 'joy': clearly schizoid. Yeats: 'glory', 'friends', 'Maud Gonne', 'Byzantium': pass me the straitjacket.

But anyway, it simply won't do to imply that Gurney's preoccupation with certain words and their meanings is obsessive and self-absorbed. Quite apart from the fact that he speaks of honour as owed 'the boys who saw a terror/Of waste, endured horror, and were not fearer' ('Mist on Meadows' – Kavanagh's version) – and where's the self-absorption in

83

speaking what is the plain truth of others' circumstances: quite apart from this, we must note that the very title of *Rewards of Wonder*, far from being a clue to Gurney's mental instability, is necessarily teasing. Whether Kipling's *Rewards and Fairies* was lodged somewhere in his mind when he chose the title for his 'poems of Cotswold, France, London' I don't know. It's possible, because he refers in 'I Saw England (July Night)', to 'Sussex tales out of Roman heights callen', which is a reference to Kipling's tales for children that bring the English past and present together, and because its interlinked poems include 'If –' and, in the expanded version, 'The Glory of the Garden'. The real rewards of wonder, Gurney may be saying from the far side of a war Kipling had welcomed, is that England is no longer a garden, or if it is, is one that has been changed by the fall, and that men who kept their heads in the most terrible war of all gain no reward for it. Or should we take 'reward' in the sense used in hunting and falconry, where it means giving hound or bird part of the carcass of the hunted quarry? If this is so, Gurney's rewards are, or anyway include, the inexpungible memories of war, of carcasses, torn and bloodied bodies, and parts of bodies.

This is speculation. More certain is that the title cuts both ways. There are rewards of wonder. There are also rewards to be wondered at. In the first sense these rewards are usually positive. In the second, where Gurney considers the rewards of war or of fighting, they are more often than not negative. In 'Glory – and Quiet Glory', a poem that comes early on in the collection, Gurney connects wonder to works of nature and art: 'Man take the heaven of glories for his own,/He limns them out and sings them on stringed wood/...To be the wonder and remind to men'. Yet there is also 'Armour scoured strictly till the man's eye wondered'. Gurney's experience of war leads to wonder of the most sceptical kind: 'the day's useless, absurd danger and hardship' he calls it in 'Laventie Dawn', which comes some three poems after 'Glory – and Quiet Glory'.

This is the key to Gurney's procedure in *Rewards of Wonder*, and to understand as much is to recognize just how extra-ordinary an effort went into making the collection. Walter says that 'By July 1924, Gurney had selected a hundred [poems], arranged them as a unified volume and given it the title of

84

"Reward of Wonder"'.[9] Unfortunately, he doesn't make any attempt to explain the arrangement or show in what way the collection *is* a unified volume. Arnold Rattenbury very helpfully offers an analogy with musical composition. There is something symphonic about *Rewards of Wonder*, he suggests. Gurney announces themes, returns to and develops them, providing something new each time. This is undoubtedly so, as the number of repeated titles implies: 'Crucifix Corner', 'First Time In', 'Tobacco', 'The Bargain', for example, all occur more than once. Moreover, places are regularly re-visited: 'Cotswold', 'Cotswold Slopes', 'Crickley', 'Crickley Morning', 'Laventie', 'Laventie Dawn', 'Laventie Front', 'Riez Bailleul', 'Riez Bailleul Also', 'Robecq', 'Robecq – A Memory', etc.

Making a unified book out of a mass of seemingly individual poems wasn't of course new. Yeats had from the beginning seen each of his collections as a thematically connected whole, and in *Responsibilities* (1914), he brought this concern for wholeness to a new level of achievement. Gurney read and much admired *Responsibilities* when Macmillan issued it in slightly enlarged form in England in 1916, and Yeats's example probably had an influence on him when he came to put together *Rewards of Wonder*. At all events, poems play off against each other with a gathering force, so much so that it's only when they are read against each other that we can fully understand Gurney's intention for the volume as a whole. This isn't to ignore, or to scant, Rattenbury's fruitful suggestion of the collection's 'symphonic' structure. It is merely to say that as a literary critic I want to try to account for the greatness of *Rewards of Wonder* in ways that will, with luck, reveal its splendours to those not helped by the musical analogy. And I should add that, given the collection's length, its richness, diversity, yet coherence, it would clearly be impossible to go through it poem by poem. What follows is, then, no more than a sketchy introduction to the way in which *Rewards of Wonder* needs to be read.

The first poem is a sonnet. 'The Lantern-Shine' evokes a spirit of lassitude or worse that Gurney throws off as he moves from lowland darkness to the Roman camp on Cotswold, 'white scarred, high in the all-healing night'. This is followed by 'October', a poem celebrating the ability to create music that comes 'out of the war of wind, earth and sky'. In contrast to this exultant creativity are 'mean men and spirits safe in homes'. In its opposition of individual creative energy to prudential values, this may feel Romantic to the point of cliché, and in the next poem, 'Glory – and Quiet Glory', Gurney reinforces the impression when he speaks of 'How much blind glory passes by sleepy heads'. But in the very next poem, it is he who, as the title has it, is 'Half Dead'. And this is not merely the fatigue that comes of physical tiredness, whether from night walking or trench wakefulness (for the poem veers between memories of Cotswold and of France); there is also 'my sick mind'.

Then comes the long 'Tobacco'. Here, Gurney praises 'The unfabled herb; the plant of peace, the known king/Of comfort bringers'. Very Chestertonian. But the poem suddenly veers to a consideration of young Gloucester soldiers, 'men talking lazily/ Smoke in luxuriously, of Woodbines, Goldflakes easily', in their caves of dugouts. Then 'Wires hang bodies for such courage as tobacco makes known – /Machine guns sweep in heaps those who such honour keep'. He means, I think, that the men who spoke of courage as they smoked and who fought honourably (or, more troublingly, fought for the honour of their country), ended up dead on the barbed wire, of no more consequence than piles of dust. And while those swept heaps remind us that all turns to dust, the particular violence of the image of machine-guns which 'sweep in heaps' Gurney's soldier-companions, reveals we have come a long way from the Cotswold night of what seemed an exuberant 'war of wind, earth and sky'. Apparently casual metaphor has deepened to terrible reality. Tobacco is a momentary stay against the horrors which issue out of 'hunger for Empire, any use of War's hammer'. This dystopic awareness is set, granite-hard, against the utopian vision of

> Tea and tobacco after decent day, body-clean labour,
> Would bring again England of madrigal, pipe, and tabor –
> Merry England again of Daniel, after four centuries,
> Of dawn rising and late talking and go-as-you-please.

Before *Rewards of Wonder* comes to its close we shall hear more of this vision, rooted as always for Gurney and many of his socialist contemporaries in that ideal Elizabethanism given most memorable utterance by R. H. Tawney. Elizabethan England is, to repeat Tawney's account, an interlude between two worlds:

'the meaningless ferocity of a feudalism turned senile...and the demure austerities of the first, pious phase of capitalism'.

Gurney will return to his shared vision of the Golden Age. But for the moment his attention has shifted to France, and so the next poem is 'Laventie Dawn', which replaces the night settings of the earlier, Cotswold, poems by 'Mud fields soiled and heavy with War's colours'. Yet even here, 'the thought of the tea cheered us boys/Who had Cotswold courage but right love for Cotswold joys', and who 'scrawl or read an hour.../Before the day's useless, absurd danger and hardship,/That began, tea, tobacco, letters – and hope showing clear'. This is how the poem ends, with hope replacing the grip of War's dolours, and with this we swing back to Cotswold and to 'Leckhampton Elbow': 'To see Cotswold cliff standing nobly to wonder/A curious walker, and ready to love – drawing music/And the hidden plain for thought'. The plain is hidden because of 'A queer unlooked for relic of short storm'. Perhaps war is a tempest that will blow itself out and leave Gurney's England still and forever a place of wonder, 'of sun's/Draping or blessing the cliffs'.

The first seven poems of *Rewards of Wonder* introduce all of the collection's major themes. Gurney makes use of weather, storm, wind, sun, times of day, times of year, light, dark, past, present, England, France, recalled war, remembered peace, boisterously imaginative men, others of sluggish stay-abed routine, to point up his turn-and-turn-again concerns. Above all, he is trying to account for the horrors of the war, the butchery of millions of men, the acquiescence of so many in England to what happened, and at the same time find justification for setting against these matters his utopian vision of a possible England, one made manifest in companionship as opposed to the private spirit, that spirit he repeatedly characterizes as soul-numbing 'politeness'. Companionship goes with tea, tobacco, bawdy talk, with song, with hospitality. Again and again he comes back to these things. And he as often comes back to their absence in a post-war England where 'folk look polite'.

These reiterated concerns cannot possibly be thought of in terms of 'monotonous regularity'. In the Whitmanesque-titled 'When The Sun Leaps Tremendous', Gurney imagines the sun bursting above the horizon and being gladdened by 'eyes of welcome'. To Whitman, then, we can add the Blake who imaged the sun as Glad Day, a principle of energy come to redeem the world, which in Blake's case, as here in Gurney's, was specifically London. And for both poets, such a sun is 'Friendly to children', that is to all who are capable of wonder, who welcome the possibilities of change.

> But City people keep shameful soft beds in brick
> And slate erections polite, set far too thick.
> Sleep because others sleep, and have regular meals –
> Not imagining how Orion or Arcturus or the Great Bear wheels.

Gurney, the inveterate night walker and star-gazer, did not like regular meals. But you don't need to know this to understand that in these lines he has in his sights what Blake memorably defined as the soft, bent bones of Londoners, those bowed under a weight of convention, seemingly incapable of throwing off the burden they had allowed to be placed on them. They, too, lived in slate erections 'polite'. There is a powerful current of wit running through Gurney's use of the word. 'Polite society' was, after all, the acme of civilized attainment. But against the villas which 'stand there and look polite – with folk polite' ('The Bargain' – they had also been targeted in 'Of Bricks and Brick Pits'), Gurney opposes life 'At The Inn', where he plays for 'twenty men willing', tunes to which they sing: 'Widdicome Fair', 'I'm Seventeen Come Sunday', 'Furze', and 'Spanish Sailors', and

> Cold left my blood, I was in desired company,
> With Bardolph's friends and Drayton's, fire comforted me,
> Blaze lit warmth; warmth moved my love's mind to more love:
> To midnight so might the talking hours, with stars above, move.

In the later 'Roads – Those Roads' and still later 'I Saw England (July Night)', the 'orange window' of the one, the 'brown-gold windows' of the other, symbolize the warmth, companionship, hospitality, which, for literary precedent, Gurney would have found in Jonson's 'To Penshurst', with its encomium to the house's 'fires/[which] Shine bright on every hearth as the desires/Of thy Penates had been set on flame'. For Gurney, whose two-thousand-year home, the Cotswolds, was, he always felt, deeply imbued with the Roman spirit or indeed spirits, the Lares and Penates, those gods of hearth and household, their emblems the welcoming lights made by fire and lantern or candle, would have been especially cherishable.

But, as we have seen, the sun's light and warmth are equally cherishable. Gurney returns to this in 'Smudgy Dawn', which he images 'scarfed with military colours'.

> Peace had the grey West fleece clouds sure in its power –
> Out on much-Severn I thought waves readied for laughter,
> And the fire-swinger promised behind the elm-pillars
> A day worthy such beginning to come after.
> To the room then to work with such hopes as may
> Come to the faithful night worker, in West Country's July.

It is impossible to unpick the literal from the metaphoric here, nor should we try to do so. This is a description of uncertain morning holding out the promise of a perfect day. It is also about how Peace can come from a necessary war against those forces symbolized by the grey fleece clouds. (That the German army wore grey doesn't mean Gurney is thinking so much of them as of vast armies of the unjust which have to be opposed and conquered.) Buoyed up by this sense that history is moving in the right direction, that after dreadful night comes Glad Day, Gurney, the faithful night-worker, can take up his own work.

The next poem returns us to war. 'Crucifix Corner' is bound to seem a piece of the work created by the night worker. In other words, it is a poem by the poet who sees himself responsible for writing about the war he has survived. It begins with an account of a line soldier's routine discomforts.

> There was a water dump there and regimental
> Carts came every day to line up and fill full
> Those rolling tanks with chlorinated clay mixture
> And curse the mud...

What breaks this routine is not, however, the to-be-expected sound of guns or 'last Trump', but a clarinet, which sings (not plays) 'Hundred Pipers and A' and 'Aveluy's pipers answered with pipers' true call/'Happy we've been a'gether', so that 'Gaiety split discipline in sixes and sevens/.... It was as if Cinderella had opened the Ball /And music put aside time's saddened clothing'. A poem which had begun with the drabness of army life thus ends in exultation. 'After music, and a day of walking or making,/To return to music, or to read the starred dark dawn-blind.'

Yet from this togetherness and the contentment which issues from it, we move in the next poem to the isolation of 'Half Dead' with its 'dysentry pangs, going blind among sleepers/And dazed into half dark'. Even here, though, the mood turns as 'the cold [brings] me sane' to see 'Whitcombe Steep as it were.../ And the clear flames of stars'. This is not so much home thoughts from abroad as a calming vision of an inviolable universe. But then comes 'Today', which plunges deep into horror: 'The unclean hells and the different Hell's terrors/That seized the heart'; and now the calming vision cannot help.

> Dreadful are the morning heavens in their lovely looks
> Mocking the hope of shaping earth's thought again,
> For men deny honour as of the spirit of their blood,
> And it is I, a war-poet, mark of the greed of evil mood,
> Whose right is of earth's requirings of Man, honour and gratitude.

From the hope of 'Smudgy Dawn' we have now moved to a black hell of despair. I don't know what the 'unclean hells' are but I suspect Gurney must have in mind sexual torment, whether his own or others', and this combines with the hell of war, of what men do to one another, to create in him a conviction that as war-poet he must record the greed of evil mood – by which I take it he means the mood's all-consuming power – rather than write about what is more conventionally required of the war-poet, 'honour and gratitude'. So at least I read this dark, tortured and tortuous poem. But it's important to note that Gurney is deeply involved in its registering of 'evil moods': it's his as much as that of other men. He, too, is marked. Moreover, it *is* mood, not settled state.

If we were in any doubt as to Gurney's ability to distinguish between these two conditions, the next poem dispels it. For 'Early Spring Dawn', a lyric which begs to be set to music, ushers in a cleansing, redemptive vision. 'Long shines the thin light of the day to north-east', it begins, 'The sun will appear, and dance, leaping with light'; and the poem closes with the discreetly joyous 'Day's dear wind is blowing'. The foulness of 'Today' is dispelled by this restorative vision of the future.

And from *this* we move to 'First Time In', a poem I considered in the previous chapter, and which I now wish to consider in the context of *Rewards of Wonder*.

After the dread tales and red yarns of the Line
Anything might have come to us; but the divine
Afterglow brought us up to a Welsh colony
Hiding in sandbag ditches, whispering consolatory
Soft foreign things. Then we were taken in
To low huts candle-lit shaded close by slitten
Oilsheets, and there but boys gave us kind welcome;
So that we looked out as from the edge of home
Sang us Welsh things, and changed all former notions
To human hopeful things. And the next days' guns
Nor any Line-pangs ever quite blot out
That strangely beautiful entry to War's rout,
Candles they gave us precious and shared over-rations –
Ulysses found little more in his wanderings without doubt.
'David of the White Rock', the 'Slumber Song' so soft, and that
Beautiful tune to which roguish words by Welsh pit boys
Are sung – but never more beautiful than here under the guns'
    noise.

The wind of 'Early Spring Dawn' has done its work. The infected vision of 'Today' has been replaced by the cleansed and cleansing vision of 'First Time In', with its heartfelt celebrations of Welsh miners, of their candle-lit world of companionship and song, which awaken Gurney and his mates out of former fears and introduce them to 'human hopeful things', so that 'War's rout' means both the noise and confusion of war and 'A large party or social gathering'. The possibilities of such a rout are, I suggest, contained in 'red yarns', for though that can be taken to mean tales of horrid mutilation ('that red, wet thing') it can as well mean tales of socialist defiance, of making a new world out of the ruins of the old one.

The Glosters first went into Line in late May, 1916, over a year before the Bolshevist uprising from which came 'To the Prussians of England'. I don't, however, mean to suggest that from the far side of war Gurney looks back to his early days in France and falsifies the record by suggesting that from the first he and his mates realized they were fighting 'the bosses' war'. For we know that many among the line soldiers were socialists (the Welsh pit boys certainly were), and 'red yarns' must therefore have been commonplace. Eric Leed quotes the German Hans Zehrer as saying that most soldiers at the front became socialists 'not because they understood Marx, but because they...felt social injustice deeply and could thus understand the justification for the social resentment that lived within the working class'.[10] This oddly suggests that most soldiers *weren't* working class, whereas of course they were. Gurney wasn't, but he came more and more to identify with his fellow soldiers, especially, though by no means exclusively, the Glosters. Hence, the letters to Marion Scott in which he delightedly reports their words, their idiomatic turns of phrase, their wit. Hence, too, 'Billet',[11] where he reports one private who 'took on himself a Company's heart to speak':

> 'I wish to bloody Hell I was just going to Brewery – surely
> To work all day (in Stroud) and be free at tea-time – allowed
> Resting when one wanted, and a joke in season,
> To change clothes and take a girl to Horsepool's turning,
> Or drink a pint at 'Traveller's Rest', and find no cloud.
> Then God and man and war and Gloucestershire would
>   have a reason,
> But I get no good in France, getting killed, cleaning off mud.'
> He spoke the heart of all of us – the hidden thought burning,
>   unturning.

In his famous poem 'my sweet old etcetera', the American poet, e. e. cummings, who had fought in France during the war's last months, thinks of how

> my
> mother hoped that
>
> i would die etcetera
> bravely of course my father used
> to become hoarse talking about how it was
> a privilege and if only he
> could meanwhile my
>
> self etcetera lay quietly
> in the deep mud et
>
> cetera
> (dreaming,
> et
>   cetera, of
> Your smile
> eyes knees and of your Etcetera)

There's an obvious link between cummings's ribaldry and the

thoughts of Gurney's private. But there's also a difference, and it's focused by that phrase 'the hidden thought burning'. 'The heart burns', Gurney says at the end of 'Strange Hells', thinking of the treatment of war veterans, the way they are devalued by the very society they fought to save. Heroism, nobility, courage: no, cummings says, they weren't on my mind when I lay in the mud. Nor did they have much to do with the thoughts engaging Gurney's mates. But if they were thinking of the girls they'd left behind, they were also conscious that, as the private says, 'I get no good in France, getting killed, cleaning off mud'. In other words, the war isn't doing any good and no good can come of it, we're fighting and getting killed for nothing we believe in or care about. That's as good a definition of a red yarn as any.

When the phrase 'red yarn' is introduced in 'First Time In' it prompts Gurney, not surprisingly, to wonder what such yarns might lead to. Court martial, perhaps? Mutiny, followed by reprisal and execution? (British troops mutinied in large numbers only after the war, but there was a widely reported French mutiny after the disaster of Neuve-Chapelle in 1917.) Coming across the Welsh pit boys, 'changed all former notions/ To human hopeful things'. Such things *must* involve a desire for change, for making a new world. That such a desire was common among line soldiers, and, *pace* Leed, was overtly political, is evident, not merely from Gurney's writing, but from that of another war-poet, Isaac Rosenberg.

Like Gurney, Rosenberg was a line soldier. Unlike Gurney, however, he had been a socialist from early days. While home on leave from the front in 1917, he read an anti-war verse play by his friend, R. C. Trevelyan, and wrote to tell him that 'The ideas are exactly what we all think out here – and the court martial of the Kaiser and kings etc. might have been copied from one of ours'. He perhaps had especially in mind some lines from the play which report that

> The streets were filled with huge crowds of civilians,
> Soldiers and sailors and munition-workers,
> All shouting, 'Down with war and the governing classes!' ...
> The censorship was paralysed, and when once
> The good news reached the trenches and the fleets
> There broke out fraternizing mutinies ...

In his important article 'Isaac Rosenberg, Revolutionary Poet',

Charles Hobday notes that Rosenberg's response to Trevelyan's play shows

> (1) that Rosenberg fully shared Trevelyan's view that not only Germany and Austria but the ruling classes of all the belligerent powers were guilty of causing the war, though in varying degrees; (2) that he had discussed this idea with his fellow-soldiers, and found that they accepted it; (3) that he believed a revolution was coming...[12]

Rosenberg was writing in September 1917, when the Bolshevik revolution in Russia was a month away. Gurney is writing some six or so years later, when further revolutions have failed to materialize. The human hopeful things have been thwarted. This is why *Rewards of Wonder* repeatedly visits Cotswold, France, London, veers between hope and despair, past and present. The volume is an attempt to understand history, to account for why matters have turned out as they have. And so in one poem, 'Clouds Die Out In June', Gurney works in hope while 'Waiting for the dawn as first mark – and more clouds of high June'. The dawn ought to usher in new life, but 'more clouds' suggest that the tremendous sun of a glad day may after all be obscured.

And so it proves. For the next poem, called 'Blighty', remembers a return from France to the England of

> Trains and restrictions, order and politeness and directions,
> Motion by black and white, guided ever about ways
> And staleness with petrol-dust distinguishing days.
> A grim faced black-garbed mother efficient and busy
> Set upon housework, worn-minded and fantasy free –
> A work-house matron, forgetting her old birth friend – the Sea.

The pun on work-house points the joylessness of a life that is without hope or dreams, which to the black-garbed mother will be mere fantasy, therefore. It's a passage of rapid notation, but brilliantly fashioned in order to indicate the sad deadness of lives run on machine-like lines, where civility and servility, order and politeness, elide. And the very next poem is 'The Bargain', with its account of 'folk-polite/Where sedges stood for the wind's play and poet-delight'. The sharp, insistent rhyme points the contrast between constraint and exuberance – in a word sameness and change – which so perplexed and distressed

Gurney. Why had this happened? Why had politeness been allowed to squeeze out delight and play? As I write the words down I think of Blake, and in particular of the Nurse in *Songs of Experience*, whose warning to her charges that 'Your spring and your day/Are wasted in play/And your winter and night/In disguise' is the very essence of sad, polite restriction. And I think of those moments or motifs in *Rewards of Wonder*, where Gurney rejoices in all forms of human behaviour – talk, song, walking, working freely – that testify to the energy which, as Blake unforgettably said, is eternal delight, and that release the capacity for wonder which ought to make possible the realization of a new world.

Gurney returns to this in 'June's Meadows', which picks up and develops the threads of meaning running through 'Clouds Die Out In June'. There, clouds threaten to return, to block out the sun. Here, the grass laid in swathes suggests to him the possibility of 'music or stories', 'Tales that a town living folk looks over' and as a result of which they will crave 'For days golden again, for the Golden Age'. The artist is charged with interpreting the natural world in a way that fleshes it out as a place of wonder and one to be attained by all – not just country folk, but those who live in towns.

Again, a comparison with Rosenberg is in order. Hobday notes that Rosenberg thought not only that a revolution was imminent but that 'imaginative literature...and perhaps his own poetry, could contribute to bring it about'.[13] In 'June's Meadows', Gurney suggests that the tales he could tell

> might bring wonder to men, and that
> Growing to action, should the will create
> For eager shaping to what Time may divine, make divine.
> But that's a strength in story denied to me...

The last line may look like a sudden moment of self-doubt, but I'm not so sure. It can after all be read to mean not so much that Gurney doubts his own ability, as that others do. He can't get his poems published. For in the previous poem, 'Poets', he begins by asking, 'Who would have thought the men who watched the stars/...Would so tamely on common custom followed/And lain all the unsurpassed night.../... so easy policed were they!' These are the folk who have learned or been forced into politeness. Unfortunately, they also happen to be poets, who have accepted 'the immemorial tame set decrees/Of bed-and-breakfast, office and life by degrees'. I've no idea who, if anyone, Gurney had in mind here, but it's safe to assume that he is writing out of angry contempt for poets he sees as having abandoned their responsibility to all that's meant by wonder.

He, however, has not.

> But one Ben Jonson honoured, and took at dawn his verses
> In London City – to meet dawn and tea-drinking apprentices:
> And take at resting his verses over tea, both virtues tasting.

Ben Jonson now becomes the poet as exemplar. Indifferent to bourgeois, prudential values, living a companionable life in taverns, or walking under the stars, he is for Gurney 'my Master, the great Ben Jonson' ('Dawn'), a creator indifferent to 'tame set decrees'. A run of poems after this one is set at early light ('Late May', 'Dawn') and between them they interweave a concern for poets and poetry ('Songs Come to the Mind', 'Buysscheure', 'The Poet Walking'). They brood over the poet's purpose, they consider the night wanderings that engender wonder, and they gather up 'poet's hopes out there; and musician's hopes'. And as hopes include responsibilities, it is surely appropriate that the next poem should be 'Strange Hells', where the poet is compelled to write of those who fought in the terrible war and who are now reduced to abject poverty, to begging, and to secretly storing thoughts of revenge, for, in this polite nation so easily policed, 'one has to keep out of face how heart burns'. The intellectual and imaginative conception of this sequence is so extraordinary, so consummate an achievement, that I can only wonder aghast at attempts to explain it away as the outpourings of a schizoid personality.

Nor does it end there. As I've said, *Rewards of Wonder* is too rich and complex to be accounted for in a few pages. In the interest of pointing to major themes and connections, I have to overlook much. Turn a few pages, therefore, and you come to the poem 'Incredible Thing', ostensibly about Cotswold's Roman past. But who can read the opening lines without considering the present?

> The mutineers, true Romans that once were Scyllas
> Had never dreamed of bijou or neat villas.

> Clear marching minds; but we are threatened with worse
> Profanation, on Man's longing a bitterer curse.

After this opening stanza, the first of three, matters become tricky. Gurney must have had a particular profanation in mind, because in the second verse he refers to how 'the sea's low soil/ Itself may be piled to cirrus for a fool's whim./Titus or Galba had never heard of such as him.' Walter suggests that the Titus Gurney has in mind was 'Titus Flavius Vespanius, the Roman general and statesman who...was Emperor of Rome between 79–81 AD'. As for Galba, that is more certainly 'Servius Sulpicius Galba, the Roman soldier and statesman who served briefly as emperor between 68 and 69 AD before being murdered by mutinous troops'.[14] Which may be so, but doesn't help resolve the question of what profanation, what bitter curse on Man's longing, Gurney has in mind. Nor does the final stanza resolve the issue, despite its compelling image of a kind of Elizabethan over-reacher 'Who'd strike the sky for bravado, and blind out the stars/But take no danger – keep clear of the hazard of dim wars'. Blind out the stars. Marlowe would have rejoiced to find that phrase for Tamburlaine. But Gurney's bully boy is a coward, who has accumulated wealth, roared on the war, but taken good care to keep out of it. Who then is he?

Horatio Bottomley MP, perhaps? Bottomley had fought the war from Fleet Street as editor of *John Bull*, denouncing pacifists as traitors. By 1922 he had been unmasked as a swindler, his Premium Bond and Victory Bond schemes, most of which were paid for out of the pockets of the poor, arrant chicanery, means to embezzle vast sums for his own use. In May 1922, he was sentenced to seven years' penal servitude. Bottomley was a nasty bastard, of a kind the political right habitually throws up. Dr Johnson's famous dictum about patriotism being the last refuge of the scoundrel certainly applies to him, although it should be noted that in his case patriotism was also the first and middle resort. Even so, I wonder whether Gurney would have thought of Bottomley as so threatening a figure, let alone one to throw a curse over Man's longing. For the generalizing insistence of that phrase can hardly be squared with Bottomley's having cheated people out of hard-earned savings. If I puzzle over this it's because the poem sounds a note which echoes in others, of a very deep disillusionment with England. Of course,

Gurney is right to speak with contempt of those who told lies about the war. He has some venomous lines on the *Daily Mail*, a newspaper which gave home readers 'news that we –/In the devil of it – could neither make guess at nor see' ('Bacon of Mornings').

The *Daily Mail* was particularly loathed by line soldiers, not merely for its hun-hating jingoism – most newspapers shared that – but for offering the hospitality of its pages to the war poems of Jessie Pope, including the infamous 'The Call':

> Who's for the trench –
> Are you, my laddie?
> Who'll follow French –
> Will you, my laddie?
> Who's fretting to begin,
> Who's going out to win?
> And who wants to save his skin –
> Do you, my laddie?

These were the verses Owen had in mind when he wrote his great poem 'Dulce et Decorum Est'. And I can well understand why, as *Rewards of Wonder* nears its end, Gurney is driven back to memories of the war, to 'Merville', 'Robecq – A Memory', 'Billet', 'Rouen', and 'Crucifix Corner', and also to a longer version of 'First Time In'. He needs these poems both because they revisit the places of actual suffering and redemption, through companionship, the dream of a new world, and because, as he winds to his close, he has to remind his readers of all the war meant to him and countless thousands of line soldiers. As he says in 'Robecq – A Memory', 'Black time takes much and hides these things away'. In common with other soldiers who survived the war, Gurney had daily experience of how, in the 1920s, war was indeed being hidden away, the events of 1914–18 tidied into an acceptable history.

This is why the next poem should be 'Possessions', which grieves over the trees that have gone from Witcombe steep, and which imagines how 'new clearings/For memory are like to weep'. Here as elsewhere, Gurney is fulfilling that function of the poet which, Wordsworth remarked, was to restore things 'silently gone out of mind and things violently destroyed'. 'War need not cut down trees', Gurney says in the same poem. But it did. At least three million of them in England alone. War destroyed the England Gurney and others were supposedly fighting to preserve. When he revised the poem, therefore, he rewrote the last lines in order to produce the plangent claim that 'It was right for the beeches to stand over Witcombe reaches,/ Until the wind roared and softened and died to sleep'. Here as elsewhere in Gurney's poetry, the word 'right' has about it a feel of absolute authority. This is a natural, unopposable right, which has nevertheless been denied.

It is for this reason that, returning to 'First Time In', he does not end on the note of quiet exultance which characterized the first statement of this theme of discovered companionship. True, he comes back to the songs sung by the Welsh pit boys, and again rejoices in the memory of the evening he shared with them. But the promise that evening held out, of a new society, has not been fulfilled. He now knows he had spent the time with

> After-War so surely hurt, disappointed men
> Who looked for the Golden Age to come friendly again.
> With inn evenings of meetings in warm glows,
> Talk: coal and wood fire uttering rosy shows
> With beer and 'Widdicombe Fair' and five miles homeward –

By the time Gurney was writing these lines, the mines had been returned to private ownership. The first act of the newly empowered owners was to lower pit wages. There had been strikes against this but they had failed and were, indeed, to go on failing, as the disaster of the 1926 General Strike would reveal. The memory of that trench evening notwithstanding, therefore, the horror of war returns next day. 'And I lay belly upward to wonder: when – but useless.' And so the poem ends, with that queer, broken-off phrase. What was he wondering? When the Golden Age might come? If so, it explains why that word 'when' is snapped off by 'but useless'. For, writing several years after the war, Gurney has to face the defeat of those hopes which the meetings of war had helped to engender and strengthen. The next poem begins 'Disappointment comes to all men'.

But there are two more poems to come before *Rewards of Wonder* is complete. 'Brimscombe' balances fatigue and pain against Gurney's ability, still, to marvel at the natural world.

Wandering at night, he sees 'the stars like candles gleam' and 'This perfect moment had such pure clemency/That it my memory has all coloured since'. Clemency? It means 'Mildness or gentleness of temper in the exercise of authority or power, mercy or leniency. Mildness of weather or climate.' Thus the *OED*. You could therefore read the poem as reporting and endorsing a visionary moment: it's a Spinozistic acceptance of the universe, of its laws. And there's no doubt that star-gazing had a steadying effect on Gurney's soul. But the poem ends with him recalling that whatever is implied by 'stars and dark eminence' was '(The thing we looked for in our fear of France)'. Held in brackets though the last line is, the move from 'I' to 'we' indicates that a yearning for all that's embodied in clemency was a collective one: the dream of mild weather, gentleness in authority, is a dream of the Golden Age, of a good society. But that the line *should* be contained within brackets makes plain the provisional nature of the dream, as though it can never be released or realized.

Yet the last poem of all refuses to settle for defeat. 'Poem for End' is also Poem for Beginning. Its seven stanzas written in rhyming triplets are so tightly inter-woven that I cannot quote from them without wrenching the developing argument in a way that distorts and maims. One reason for this is that Gurney so tightly braids together references to war-time France and Cotswold – to Severn and Somme as it were – that, as he says, 'the wrought out links/Of fancy to fancy' out of which he has made both poems and music represent both 'a book ended' and a 'heart aching'. Moreover, he is, he insists, 'A war poet whose right of honour cuts falsehood like a knife'. This takes us back to the image which so disturbed Marion Scott when Gurney introduced it into 'To the Prussians of England'. Now, he develops it. Here are the poem's final stanzas.

> War poet – his right is of nobler steel – the careful sword –
> And night walker will not suffer of praise the word
> From the sleepers; the custom-followers, the dead lives
> unstirred.
>
> Only, who thought of England as two thousand years
> Must keep of today's life, the proper anger and fears,
> England that was paid for by building and ploughing and tears.

The sword is at once the sword of honour (true honour, not the mouth honour uttered by those whom soldiers learnt to distrust and despise), the sword of justice, and of vengeance. Gurney's contempt for the sleepers, for those timid souls immured in their villas and polite lives, who have chosen not to awaken to 'proper anger and fears', is as absolute as his identification with an England 'paid for by building and ploughing and tears'. When Adam delved and Eve span/Who was then the gentleman? John Ball's question is at the heart of the utopian vision of a sweet, equal republic which Morris so eagerly embraced, and it is implicit in Gurney's sense of an England 'paid for by building and ploughing and tears'. *This* England was created, as Edward Thomas said, by 'the actual, troublous life of every day and toil of the hands and brain together'. Building and ploughing: industrial and agricultural, it may be, whose apt symbols could even be taken as the hammer and sickle. At all events, Gurney's great volume ends, not with defeat, but with his self-imposed resolution, his declaration of intent. The true poet must bear witness, must keep 'of today's life, the proper anger and fears'. The poem's last lines recall the 'fierce indignation' of 'Sonnet. September 1922', but in their linking of fears and tears they also voice a necessary doubt about the possibility of achieving the Golden Age which Gurney and his soldier comrades had imagined or dared to hope might be waiting for them and for which, indeed, they were fighting. For what else could justify their sufferings, the endless killing, maiming, maddening of millions?

III

Like John Clare's great volume *A Midsummer Cushion, Rewards of Wonder* was not to be published in the poet's lifetime. Locked away in Dartford, Gurney nevertheless went on writing, as over half a century earlier Clare had in Northampton Asylum. And, like Clare, Gurney had only the past out of which to make his poems. Not surprisingly, the past which most haunted him was war-time France. Out of that past stepped 'The Bohemians', his comic-affectionate recall of the awkward squad, those 'who would not clean their buttons,/Nor polish buckles after the

101

latest fashions,/Preferred their hair long, puttees comfortable/
... In Artois or Picardy they lie – free of useless fashions'.
Gurney plainly loves these natural dissidents, the natural
successors to those inhabitants of Eastcheap he so warmed to
when he came across them in Shakespeare's great tetralogy
of English history which is, among much else, a dramatization of
the costs of war. War makes heroes. It also makes victims of
those caught up in it through no fault of their own. At the end of
Henry IV Part One, Falstaff says of the men he pressed into
service, 'I have led my ragamuffins where they are pepper'd;
there's not three of my hundred and fifty left alive, and they are
for the town's end, to beg during life'. Impossible not to imagine
how the poet who had written 'Strange Hells' would respond to
Falstaff's casual brutality. Nor how he would have been moved
by the words of that line soldier, Williams, who, seizing on the
remark by his friend, Bates, that it were better for the king to be
ransomed because that way 'many poor men's lives' would be
saved, adds that if the cause for which they are fighting

> be not good, the King himself hath a heavy reckoning to make when
> all those legs and arms and heads, chopp'd off in battle, shall join
> together at the latter day and cry all 'We died at such a place' – some
> swearing, some crying for a surgeon, some upon their wives left
> poor behind them, some upon the debts they owe, some upon their
> children rawly left. I am afeared there are few die well that die in a
> battle; for how can they charitably dispose of anything when blood is
> their argument? Now, if these men do not die well, it will be a black
> matter for the King that led them to it; who to disobey were against
> all proportion of subjection. (Henry V, Act 4, scene 1).

I've no doubt that by mid 1917 Gurney had come to think the
cause no good. A late poem, 'Portrait of a Coward', very
remarkably takes the side of a soldier who couldn't cope with
life (and death) in the trenches.

> Everybody was glad – (but determined to hide the bad)
> When he took courage at wire mending and shot his leg,
> And got to Blighty, no more saying word of denying.

Bates and Williams would, *Henry V* shows, willingly hide the
bad. To be sure, they do not realize they are talking to the king
himself, who has come among them in disguise. Had they
known the true identity of the man they believe to be a common

soldier, they would almost certainly have bitten their tongues. But in the greatest of his poems about the awkward squad, Gurney certainly knows he is talking to an officer when he refuses to make a sacrificial hero of himself.

THE SILENT ONE

Who died on the wires, and hung there, one of two –
Who for his hours of life had chattered through
Infinite lovely chatter of Bucks accent;
Yet faced unbroken wires; stepped over, and went,
A noble fool, faithful to his stripes – and ended.
But I weak, hungry, and willing only for the chance
Of line – to fight in the line, lay down under unbroken
Wires, and saw the flashes, and kept unshaken.
Till the politest voice – a finicking accent, said:
'Do you think you might crawl through there; there's a hole';
                In the afraid
Darkness, shot at; I smiled, as politely replied –
'I'm afraid not, Sir.' There was no hole, no way to be seen,
Nothing but chance of death, after tearing of clothes
Kept flat, and watched the darkness, hearing bullets whizzing –
And thought of music – and swore deep heart's deep oaths.
(Polite to God –) and retreated and came on again.
Again retreated – and a second time faced the screen.

I give here the text as printed in Walter's Everyman and I do so with some misgivings, because the version printed in Kavanagh, which omits the half-line 'In the afraid' and has more sensible punctuation, seems to me preferable. On the other hand, we have to accept that Walter reproduces the text which Gurney finally approved. Kavanagh put the poem in the section he dates 1919–22. Walter no doubt accurately dates it to 1925–6. In other words, it was written at a time when Gurney was officially mad. But it is of course a deeply sane poem. More important, it is a poem about Gurney (in an early draft he even has the officer name him) or any line soldier who refuses to die pointlessly, to make an 'heroic sacrifice' in what was becoming increasingly known as the 'bosses' war'. The oxymoron 'noble fool' cruelly catches the pointlessness of such sacrifice, and this points the contrast between the soldier's 'infinite lovely chatter' and the 'finicking accent' of that officer who belongs to the world of politeness, with all the resonances we have seen that word to possess for Gurney.

'Chatter' also has its resonances. In his letters Gurney often reports on the 'chatter' of the soldiers he's among. Chatter is a token of the free spirit, the unconstrained speech of those who are not persuaded by the need to speak politely. Gurney is with the chatterers, and his bolshie refusal to obey orders comes from a sardonic, sure sense that he sees no virtue in obeying orders that will leave him, too, hanging on the wires.

'The Silent One' came in a great burst of creative activity, in which, during a period stretching from early 1925 to the middle of the following year, Gurney wrote enough poems to make up numerous volumes, plus a play, some prose, and much music. A few of the poems were published at intervals by J. C. Squire in his journal, *London Mercury*. And here it should be said that Squire, often dismissed as a literary hack, deserves all possible praise for staying true to his perception of Gurney's worth.

Some of Gurney's songs also saw the light of day, notably the cycle *The Western Playland (and of sorrow)*, published in 1926, but as the years wore on he not surprisingly sank deeper into lethargy and delusion. Like Clare before him, he imagined himself into the skin of successful writers. Clare had thought of himself as Byron. Gurney believed himself to be Shakespeare and Ben Jonson. He also claimed to be Beethoven and Haydn.

In 1932 Helen Thomas visited him and learnt that 'he refused to go into the grounds of the asylum. It was not his idea at all of the countryside – the fields and woods and footpaths he loved so well – and he would have nothing to do with this travesty of something that was sacred to him.' On her next visit she therefore took with her Edward Thomas's own much used ordnance maps of Gloucestershire.

> This proved to have been a sort of inspiration, for Ivor Gurney at once spread them on his bed and he and I spent the whole time I was there tracing with our fingers the lanes and byeways and villages of which he knew every step and over which Edward had walked. He spent that hour in re-visiting his beloved home, in spotting a village or a track, a hill or a wood and seeing it all in his mind's eye, a mental vision sharper and more actual for his heightened intensity.[15]

He had much earlier grieved over his separation from his native Cotswolds, in a poem called 'What Evil Coil' which Hurd and, following him, Kavanagh, assigned to the asylum years.

What evil coil of fate has fastened me
Who cannot move to sight, whose bread is sight,
And in nothing has more bare delight
Than dawn or the violet or the winter tree.
Stuck-in-the-mud – Blinkered up, roped for the fair.
What use to vessel breath that lengthens pain?
O but the empty joys of wasted air
That blow on Crickley and whimper wanting me!

This is not a poem of madness. Roped up as an animal bound for the fair Gurney may be, hapless and disgruntled, on the treadmill routine of the London charivari. But I don't see why we should not take that Stuck-in-the-mud literally. And if this is so, then the poem, which anyway was written before September 1922, becomes an eloquent, rending protest at trench warfare in which he, as so many others, is treated as a sacrificial animal.

It could be said that the long, embittering and ultimately soul-destroying years of his incarceration made Gurney into a sacrificial animal. In 1937 Marion Scott, with the encouragement of the composers Gerald Finzi and Howard Ferguson, who had never met Gurney but who hugely admired his work as composer, managed to persuade the editors of *Music and Letters* to devote a large part of the January 1938 issue to an appreciation of his music. Oxford University Press agreed to publish twenty of his songs in two-volume format. By now, however, pulmonary tuberculosis was running through Gurney's body. Proof copies of *Music and Letters* were sent to him, but Hurd says that he was too weak even to take the wrapping off the parcel. 'It is too late', he said. He died at 3.45 on the morning of 26 December 1937.

'It is too late'. No, but it's certainly high time for him to be recognized as not merely what he rightly called himself, '*first war poet*', meaning its best, but as one of the finest poets of the twentieth century.

Notes

CHAPTER 1. BECOMING A POET

1. Paul Fussell, *The Great War and Modern Memory* (London: Oxford University Press, 1975), 272 and 283.
2. *Severn & Somme and War's Embers*, ed. R. K. R. Thornton (Ashington, Northumberland: MidNAG; Manchester: Carcanet, 1997), 114–15.
3. See George W. Howgate, *George Santayana* (New York: Barnes & Co., 1961), 923.
4. T. Baldwin, *G. E. Moore* (London: Routledge, 1990), 129.

CHAPTER 2. 1919–1922

1. Arnold Rattenbury, 'How the Sanity of Poets Can Be Edited Away', *London Review of Books*, vol. 21, no. 20 (14 October 1999), 17.
2. *Best Poems and The Book of Five Makings*, ed. R. K. R. Thornton and George Walter (Ashington, Northumberland: MidNAG; Manchester: Carcanet, 1995), 2.
3. Rattenbury, 'How the Sanity of Poets Can Be Edited Away', 17.
4. See *Uncommon People: Resistance, Rebellion and Jazz* (London: Abacus, 1999, 175–6).
5. For which see *The Last Country Houses* (London: Yale University Press, 1982), esp. 244–52.
6. Jan Marsh, *Back to the Land: The Pastoral Movement in Victorian Britain* (London: Quartet, 1982), 102.
7. Henry Pelling, *A History of British Trade Unionism* (Harmondsworth: Pelican Original, 1963), 165.
8. See *Critical Survey*, vol. 11, no. 3 (1999), 68.
9. John Lucas, *The Radical Twenties: Aspects of Writing, Politics and Culture* (Nottingham: Five Leaves Publications, 1997; New Brunswick, NJ: Rutgers University Press, 1999), see esp. 186–7.

CHAPTER 3. THE LATER YEARS

1. D. H. Lawrence, *Selected Essays* (Harmondsworth: Penguin, 1961), 120.
2. Ibid., 119.
3. Jeremy Hooker, *Poetry of Place: Essays and Reviews, 1970–1981* (Manchester: Carcanet, 1982), 126.
4. Eric Leed, *No Man's Land: Combat and Identity in World War I* (Cambridge: Cambridge University Press, 1979), 187.
5. Ibid., 189.
6. Ibid., 187. The quotation is from Gibbs's novel *Now It Can Be Told.*
7. Ibid., 207.
8. *80 Poems or So*, ed. George Walter and R. K. R. Thornton (Ashington, Northumberland: MidNAG; Manchester: Carcanet, 1997), 12.
9. *Rewards of Wonder*, ed. George Walter (Ashington, Northumberland: MidNAG; Manchester: Carcanet, 2000), 5.
10. Leed, *No Man's Land*, 198.
11. *Rewards of Wonder*, ed. Walter, 92.
12. Charles Hobday, 'Isaac Rosenberg, Revolutionary Poet', *London Magazine*, vol. 40, nos. 3–4 (June–July 2000), 51–2.
13. Ibid., 52.
14. *Rewards of Wonder*, ed. Walter, 139.
15. Helen Thomas in the RCM (Royal College of Music) magazine, 1960, as quoted by Michael Hurd, *The Ordeal of Ivor Gurney* (Oxford: Oxford University Press, 1974), 168.

Select Bibliography

BIBLIOGRAPHIES

There is as far as I am aware no full bibliography of Gurney's poetic output, let alone his entire *oeuvre*, musical or literary. However, items appears from time to time in the *Ivor Gurney Society Journal*.

EDITIONS OF GURNEY'S POETRY

Poems by Ivor Gurney, edited with a memoir by Edmund Blunden (London: Hutchinson, 1954; o.p.).

Poems of Ivor Gurney, edited with bibliographical note by Leonard Clark (London: Chatto & Windus, 1973; o.p.). Rather fuller and better than Edmund Blunden's selection.

Collected Poems of Ivor Gurney, edited by P. J. Kavanagh (Oxford: Oxford University Press, 1982; o.p.). The nearest we have to a proper collected edition. It is now out of print. Despite the fact that Kavanagh omitted some important poems and, as subsequent research has shown, was not always correct in his dating of poems – for which he is hardly to be blamed – this edition is well worth hunting down. Kavanagh provides helpful notes and his lengthy Introduction is quite simply superb, one of the very best things so far written about Gurney. Kavanagh's edition was followed by a *Selected*, now also out of print.

The following editions of Gurney's work are highly recommended for their textual accuracy and helpful notes.

Best Poems and The Book of Five Makings, edited by R. K. R. Thornton and George Walter (Ashington: MidNAG; Manchester: Carcanet, 1995). However, the ordering of the poems, which is conjecturable, is highly questionable.

Ivor Gurney, edited by George Walter (London: Dent/Everyman, 1996).

Slim though it is, this is to be recommended for the reliability of text and dating of poems.

Severn & Somme and War's Embers, edited by R. K. R. Thornton (Ashington: MidNAG; Manchester: Carcanet, 1997).

80 Poems or So, edited by George Walter & R. K. R. Thornton (Ashington: MidNAG; Manchester: Carcanet, 1997).

Rewards of Wonder, edited by George Walter (Ashington: MidNAG; Manchester: Carcanet, 2000).

LETTERS

Ivor Gurney: Collected Letters, edited by R. K. R. Thornton (Ashington: MidNAG; Manchester: Carcanet, 1991). The annotation isn't always as full or reliable as it might be, but this pioneering edition is nevertheless of importance to any student of Gurney.

Stars in a Dark Night, edited by Anthony Boden (Gloucester: Allan Sutton, 1986). A collection of Gurney's letters to the Chapman family. This contains a number of worthwhile photographs, including one of Gurney in the 2/5 Glosters Regiment Band, taken in 1915, in which he carries what seems to be a euphonium. According to Boden, in 1914 Gurney's attachment to Kitty, the oldest of the Chapman daugters, developed 'into an emotion much deeper than affection. He approached Mr Chapman but was told, albeit kindly, that at seventeen Kitty was much too young to consider engagement'.

BIOGRAPHY

The only biography to date is that by Michael Hurd. A full-dress biography by R. K. R. Thornton is promised.

Hurd, Michael, *The Ordeal of Ivor Gurney* (Oxford: Oxford University Press, 1978). This is now seriously out of date and is, besides, written by someone who has not much understanding of poetry.

Silkin, Jon, *Gurney*, a play (North Shields: Iron Press, 1985). This is not a factually accurate account of Gurney but does speculate interestingly about his war years.

Ivor Gurney Society Journal. Publishes valuable articles.

CRITICAL STUDIES

Mine is the first monograph devoted to Gurney. All other writings on him are fugitive or contained in books which are largely about others or are comparatively short essays. Kavanagh's fine account apart, the following may be recommended:

Hill, Geoffrey: 'Gurney's Hobby', in *Essays in Criticism*, vol. XXXIV, no. 2 (April 1984).

Hooker, Jeremy, *Poetry of Place: Essays and Reviews, 1970–1981* (Manchester: Carcanet, 1982). Contains an essay called 'Honouring Ivor Gurney', pp. 120–29 which valuably identifies Gurney's regard for place.

Lucas, John, *Modern English Poetry: From Hardy to Hughes* (London: Batsford, 1985), 92–102. Considers Gurney together with other poets of the Great War.

———— 'Poetry and Politics in the 1920s', in *Poetry and Politics*, edited by Kate Flint for the English Association (Ipswich: D. S. Brewer, 1996), 84–110. This essay takes Gurney's post-war poetry and links it to that of Edgell Rickword, another poet-survivor of the war and another whose politics developed in a radical direction in the 1920s.

———— *The Radical Twenties: Aspects of Writing, Politics and Culture* (Nottingham: Five Leaves Publications, 1997; New Brunswick, NJ: Rutgers University Press, 1999). The chapter on 'Poetry, Civilisation, Culture and the Masses' (pp. 175–217 revisits the above essay).

———— 'Edward Thomas, Ivor Gurney and English Socialism', *The Ivor Gurney Society Journal*, 1998, 19–34. Relates Gurney to the work of some contemporaries, above all, Thomas, and identifies both poets as belonging to the developing utopian socialism most eloquently advanced by William Morris and, after him, R. H. Tawney.

Rattenbury, Arnold: 'How the Sanity of Poets Can Be Edited Away', *London Review of Books*, vol. 21, no. 20 (14 October 1999), 15–19. An article of the first importance which convincingly argues that much of Gurney's best writing, especially about the war, was done when he was supposedly mad. Rattenbury is also clear as to Gurney's radical imagination.

Silkin, Jon, *Out of Battle: The Poetry of the Great War* (Oxford: Oxford University Press, 1978). Silkin's brief discussion of Gurney, which runs over pp. 120–129, importantly points to his anger at the conduct of the war.

Underhill, Hugh, 'Beauty in Usuality: Ivor Gurney and the Twistedness of things', in *Critical Survey*, vol. 11, no. 3 (1999). Very acute essay on Gurney as a member of the awkward squad.

OTHER RELEVANT WORKS

Aslet, Clive, *The Last Country Houses* (London: Yale University Press, 1982). Has an important section on Detmar Blow, an architect influenced by Ruskin and the Arts and Crafts Movement, whose house in rural Gloucestershire, 'Hilles', was intended to provide a model of communal living.

Clark, K., *The Muse Colony: Dymock, 1914* (Bristol: Redcliffe Press, 1992). Useful if critically and historically naïve account of the colony of poets with whom Gurney became acquainted, and for one of whom, Wilfrid Gibson, he had a high regard.

Grant, Joy, *Harold Monro and The Poetry Bookshop* (London: Routledge & Kegan Paul, 1967). Useful account of the literary milieu in London in the years immediately before the First World War.

Graves, Robert and Alan Hodge, *The Long Weekend: A Social History of Great Britain, 1918–1938* (London: Faber, 1941). Contains much of interest and relevance, including a good account of Horatio Bottomley and his nefarious doings, pp. 76–80.

Greensted, Mary, *The Arts and Crafts Movement in the Cotswolds* (Stroud: Allan Sutton, 1993). Good survey of the kinds of utopian and other radical communities in existence in Gurney's Cotswolds.

Harvey, F. W. *Collected Poems, 1912–1957* (Coleford: D. McLean, The Forest Bookshop, 1982). The poems of Gurney's first poet-friend, including a clutch of war poems, several written while he was a p.o.w.

Hobday, Charles, 'Isaac Rosenberg, Revolutionary Poet', *London Magazine*, vol. 40, nos 3/4, pp. 42–56. Important essay which shows how widespread was radical thinking and activity among Gurney's generation.

Hobsbawm, Eric, 'Socialism and the Avant-Garde', in *Uncommon People: Resistance, Rebellion and Jazz* (London: Abacus, 1999) 171–86. Hobsbawm offers a valuable survey of the connections between advanced political and artistic thought of the period.

Lawrence, D. H., *Selected Essays* (Harmondsworth: Penguin, 1961). Contains his great essay on Nottingham and the mining villages, in which he mourns the destruction of beauty and its replacement by an ugliness that's both spiritual and physical.

Leed, Eric, *No Man's Land: Combat and Identity in World War I* (Cambridge: Cambridge University Press, 1979). A crucially important study, not least for its careful account of 'Neuroses and War'.

Marsh, Jan, *Back to the Land: The Pastoral Movement in Victorian Britain.* (London: Quartet, 1982). Despite the title, Marsh's useful survey takes in the earlier years of the twentieth century and has much of relevance to say about Cotswold communities.

Mowat, C. L., *Britain Between The Wars, 1918–1940* (London: Methuen, 1955). This magnificent book, although now nearly fifty years old, is still the best social history of its period. Essential reading.

Parker, Rennie, *The Georgian Poets* (Plymouth: Northcote House, 1999). Excellent brief survey of poets, including some close to Gurney.

Spicer, Paul, *Herbert Howells* (Bridgend: Seren, 1998). A good, brief account of a composer who was a close friend of Gurney's and who shared many of his tastes and convictions.

Smith, Stan, *Edward Thomas* (London: Faber, 1986). First-class critical study of the poet who meant so much to Gurney; Smith is good on Thomas's political ideas and his debt to William Morris.

Street, S., *The Dymock Poets* (Bridgend: Seren Books, 1994). Useful for biographical information.

Tawney, R. H., *The Radical Tradition* (Harmondsworth: Penguin, 1966). These essays, mostly first published in the first twenty years of the twentieth century, are crucially important in their ardently socialistic arguments, from history, for the achievement of a good, socialist society.

Townsend, Frances, *The Laureate of Gloucestershire: The Life and Work of F. W. Harvey, 1888–1957* (Bristol: Redcliffe Press, 1988). Enthusiastic account, which has something to say about Gurney's part in Harvey's life.

Winter, Denis, *Death's Men: Soldiers of the Great War* (Harmondsworth: Penguin, 1979). There are literally thousands of books about the Great War, but this account of the experiences of line-soldiers, mostly based on their own accounts, is an outstandingly good example.

Wolff, Leon, *In Flanders Fields: The 1917 Campaign* (London: Longman, 1959; Harmondsworth: Penguin, 1979). A good, popular account of the year-long campaign through much of which Gurney fought until he was invalided out after being gassed.

Index

113